AF572237

Joseph Ciminera's
New American Cooking
Taste This T.V.!
There are no rules in cooking

ISBN: 987-0-942407-79-2

10 9 8 7 6 5 4 3 2 1
Manufactured in the United States of America

FATHER & SON
PUBLISHING, INC.
4909 N. Monroe Street
Tallahassee, Florida 32303
800-741-2712
http://fatherson.com
e-mail lance@fatherson.com

Acknowledgements

This book would not be possible without the help and the continued loyal support of these great professional people:

First off, I would like to thank my wife Carmela, who waited many long hours for me to come home after feeding the masses in the restaurant — only to have me sit behind the computer to finish up this book. You are a true inspiration and supporter of my work. Thank you.

Many thanks go out to my family: Mom, Dad, grandmothers and grandfathers for imparting in me the knowledge of great Italian cuisine from a very early age. I would also like to thank my brothers for their continued support.

My deepest respect extends to Bryan Naylor, who has been by my side to help us strive for success; he has not had much sleep either. I must also acknowledge his wife Meagan — who has helped with many graphic projects over the years — and his grandfather.

Thanks to Peter Mantone for testing, editing and fine-tuning these recipes in an untiring fashion, with late hours in the kitchen.

To Master Chef Vincenzo Provino, a chef who believed in me and made me what I am today. From the first day that I walked into his kitchen in Italy, he treated me with nothing but respect. A true teacher — may he rest in peace.

To Sirio Maccioni, owner of Le Cirque and — in my opinion — "one of the world's greatest restauranteurs." The little time I spent working there changed the way I think about the industry.

To Julia Child: Her advice helped me through the many obstacles of television. Her memory will last forever.

To talented chefs: Oliver Keegan, Peter Hennesy, John Gilian, Armando Alicia, Anthony Silvesrti, James Muer, Brian Fishman, Pierre Manor, John McHearen, Gerry Manqué, Fritz Smith, Mike Donato, Steven Glenn, Joe Risso, Eddie Michaels, Keith Carcone, Michelle Finestra, Holly Ginnens, Chris Dolores, Sue Torres, Jody Mayo, Chris Teretto and Frank Keller.

To Richard Plutzer for matching wines with the recipes in this book and for all the support over the years with various projects.

To Julie Byun for all the help with the website.

To Ron Rosenbuam and Gary Press for always finding me hot jobs.

To Anthony Cinicola — executive banquet chef at Le Cirque 2000 — who is a true friend and a talented chef.

To Maria Bacarella, a professional food photographer who has been at my events and filmings since the beginning.

To Helen and Tom Meyers: Thanks to their crops on a small farm in Ohio, I have pleased many bellies with their produce.

To Yvette Somekh — my first television producer — who gave me a shot on television. One rainy afternoon in a small studio in Hampton, New York, the dream became a reality.

To the many sponsors who have supported me over the years in television, fund-raisers and events: Scott Sommerfield, Richard Plutzer, Charlie Whyte, Kim Delefromoy, Chef Revival, Dave Scheiber, Filippo Berio olive oil, Blendtec, Blue Q gum, Bolla wine, Bone Suckin' Sauce, Brazilian Gourmet, Cooking with Chef John, Michael's Restaurant, Buffet Enhancements, Cambro USA, Casa DiLisio, Chris Pappas, Dairyland, Bill Hodge, Steve Cast, Jeff Tantillo, Cocktail Candy, Cuisipro, D'Artagnan, De Cecco pasta, Dell'Amore, Denby Pottery, Eden Foods, Edgecraft, Evo Grill, Molinari sambuca, Mario Massina from MgM Gold Communications for all of his support with national and international companies, Idaho Trout, Jeremiah's Pick Coffee, John Boos, John Macy's CheeseSticks, Loacker, Melissa's Produce, Nueske Farm Meats, Phillips crabmeat, Ravenscroft Crystal, Renaissance Farms, Roth Käse, Teaosophy, ThermoSafe, Village Craft, Cinders Grill, Voss Water, Wells' Dairy, Wüstof Knives, All-Clad, New Wave Seafood, Tom the Nook, Waring and Tonton sauce.

Special thanks go to Scott Sommerfield for his talents with the camera and to the staff at the Crescent Beach Club for supplying me with their test kitchen.

Introduction

The successful preparation of any extensive dish is within the ability of just about everyone. Keep in mind that there are no set recipes and that they can be added to and changed according to the availability of ingredients or to suit one's taste. Remember: There are no rules in cooking. However, it's important to familiarize yourself with basic techniques and preparations.

Thanks to the help of our wonderful importers, Americans can buy anything from anywhere in the world. With that in mind, it helps make a creative, wonderful dish without having to go to Europe or a four-star restaurant. Items like antibiotic free-range pork and chicken or healthy organic produce are readily available at your grocer's market. There are many good companies that can provide you access to feeding your body the most wholesome foods this precious Earth can give you. I would like to share what has taken me years of exploration to find. Go to the back of this book for a reference guide that will have websites for all these great companies.

In my 20 years in this business, I have come to realize that the "right" recipes are the ones that you feel are good. Meaning, if you start to cook a bad meal with horrible ingredients, chances are that the recipe will not come out like you planned, and you will feel that disappointment. The best way to start off a recipe is for you to obtain and be ready and able to work with the best, freshest ingredients available. Remember my old saying: "There are no rules in cooking." I promise that I will help you learn some very basic important techniques in cooking. You will be able to create something that you have a passionate respect for. The one thing that I cannot give you, however, is the satisfaction that comes from you creating that dish; this comes from your heart. It's also a prize that you well deserve.

Always read a recipe twice, making certain that you understand the directions. You'll find it pays to look ahead, knowing what's to come. Check to make sure that you have all the necessary ingredients and equipment. You'll also want to know that you like the ingredients called for and that they meet any special dietary needs. Read to be sure you have enough time to prepare and cook the recipe.

Importantly, check for an ingredient that might be used more than once at another stage of the recipe. You don't want to mistakenly use the ingredient all at once. Of course, you'll want to know whether the oven needs to be preheated and what the recipe's yield is. All measurements are for level amounts.

Meats should be well-trimmed and free of any membranes, veins or any part that interferes with a comfortable, palatable experience.

Vegetables should be washed with plenty of clean cold water. Always remember to change the water often and scrub when necessary. Leafy produce should be trimmed of any unwanted color.

The scales, fins, skin and gills on all fish should be carefully inspected. The eyes should be clear, not cloudy. Fish intestines need to be cleaned and removed immediately.

Some foods — especially steaks and birds — should be marinated before cooking for maximum flavor. The latest fad right now is the raw vegetable diet. Some vegetables that are almost always cooked are just as good raw. Through experimentation, I'm sure you'll find that juicing vegetables and reducing them makes great sauces for certain dishes.

Importantly, the recipes in this book make 6 servings, unless otherwise specified. Wherever mentioned, butter is always unsalted. I use kosher salt or a specialty salt from Renaissance Farms in my cooking and in these recipes. Heavy cream is always 40 percent.

The food and recipes in this book have been produced by people with a passion and a creative eye for food. A good deal of focus is on artful dish composition and presentation. After all, eye appeal sets the stage in anticipation of a satisfying meal.

Recipes in this book are an example of a wide range of possibilities for what you can do with food. The style of cuisine is New American with a European flair. That basically covers all the classics of American and European cuisine, transforming it to my personal style.

Watch a person as food is placed in front of him or her. You'll see the amazing reaction. People are eager to dig in to the anticipated meal that they so crave. When food arrives, it's not uncommon for diners to break out in smiles. They look at the plate, gazing at the colors as if in a trance. Seconds later, they taste the food and react.

Anticipation and reaction will determine their attitude for the rest of the evening. So, there is a psychology to food that is science in and of itself. Give someone great-tasting food — and he or she will be extremely happy.

Hors d'oeuvres are mini-size treats that can be served and eaten hot or cold before a meal starts. They should whet the appetite for the well-anticipated meal to come, not ruin it. However, there are buffets that exclusively serve these bite-sized treats by themselves. Most times, hors d'oeuvres are eaten without a fork. They are best served and eaten with a toothpick or one's fingers.

You'll want your hors d'oeuvres to be colorful and appetizing, with a presentation as pleasing to the eye as to the palate.

First, a few suggestions: Always use the freshest, brightest vegetables available and, when you need butter or olive oil, be sure to only use sweet butter and extra virgin olive oil. I only stock Filippo Berio olive oil in my kitchen.

Fresh herbs are always preferred, but if you must, you can substitute dried. Remember that dried seasonings are often more potent (as long as they haven't been stored in your pantry too long), so you'll use a lesser amount than fresh herbs.

Finally, a few words about Parmigiano-Reggiano cheese: Produced in the Emilia-Romagna region, this is considered the king of cheeses in Italy. There, "parmesan" means Parmigiano-Reggiano cheese. Elsewhere, like here in the United States, it's usually a poor substitute for the real thing, not authentic Parmigiano-Reggiano cheese.

Always purchase this cheese ungrated and in small wedges — according to your usage frequency — for longer flavor maintenance. Look for the vertically stenciled and repeated words Parmigiano-Reggiano all around the cheese rind. This is just one of the ways you know that you are purchasing authentic Parmigiano-Reggiano cheese. Every piece of cheese cut from the wheel will have this marking on its rind.

Contents

Joseph
C.E.C.

Hors d'oeuvres are mini-size treats that can be served and eaten hot or cold before a meal starts. They should whet the appetite for the well-anticipated meal to come, not ruin it. However, there are buffets that exclusively serve these bite-sized treats by themselves. Most times, hors d'oeuvres are eaten without a fork. They are best served and eaten with a toothpick or one's fingers.

You'll want your hors d'oeuvres to be colorful and appetizing, with a presentation as pleasing to the eye as to the palate.

First, a few suggestions: Always use the freshest, brightest vegetables available and, when you need butter or olive oil, be sure to only use sweet butter and extra virgin olive oil. I only stock Filippo Berio olive oil in my kitchen.

Fresh herbs are always preferred, but if you must, you can substitute dried. Remember that dried seasonings are often more potent (as long as they haven't been stored in your pantry too long), so you'll use a lesser amount than fresh herbs.

Finally, a few words about Parmigiano-Reggiano cheese: Produced in the Emilia-Romagna region, this is considered the king of cheeses in Italy. There, "parmesan" means Parmigiano-Reggiano cheese. Elsewhere, like here in the United States, it's usually a poor substitute for the real thing, not authentic Parmigiano-Reggiano cheese.

Always purchase this cheese ungrated and in small wedges — according to your usage frequency — for longer flavor maintenance. Look for the vertically stenciled and repeated words Parmigiano-Reggiano all around the cheese rind. This is just one of the ways you know that you are purchasing authentic Parmigiano-Reggiano cheese. Every piece of cheese cut from the wheel will have this marking on its rind.

Hors d'oeuvres

Potato Blini

1 pound Idaho potatoes
2 tablespoons bread flour, sifted
1 tablespoon cake flour, sifted
3 tablespoons crème fraiche
2 large brown eggs
2 egg yolks
2 tablespoons sweet butter
¼ teaspoon Dijon mustard
salt and pepper to taste

For the blini: Clean the potatoes before baking them in a 350 degree oven until fully cooked — approximately 45 minutes to an hour. When cooled enough to handle, cut open the potatoes, scrape the flesh into a bowl and then discard the skin. Press the potatoes through a China cap strainer to break up any large lumps. Using a paddle on a stand mixer, add the mustard and flour into the potatoes, blending well. Add the crème fraiche. Increase the speed to stir quickly. Add the cake flour, continuing to mix thoroughly. Reduce the speed, slowly add the egg yolks one at a time and then continue to mix. Add the whole eggs all at once. Put the mixture in a squeeze bottle.

For cooking blini: In a nonstick pan on medium heat, melt some butter. Reduce to low heat. Squeeze half-dollar circles of the batter into the pan. Cook on both sides for at least 1 minute, but do not overbrown. The blini will rise — a sign of being fully cooked. Adjust for salt and pepper as needed.

For the plate: Blini are traditionally served with caviar. However, I like to serve them as appetizers or as hors d'oeuvres, with toppings ranging from caponata to caramelized onions and goat cheese. I find them especially delicious when the blini and topping are still good and warm. Be creative: Try a range of items from tart to sweet. Remember: There are no rules in cooking.

Chef's note: Crème fraiche is a slightly tart, raw cream that is favored in France. Unfortunately, it's not easily found in many supermarkets. But here is how you can make your own: In a small bowl, whisk 1 cup heavy cream together with 1 cup sour cream. Cover with plastic wrap. Place the mixture in a warm, dark place for 12 hours. Stir. Refrigerate for another 24 hours before serving. Eat and be happy!

Makes 25 blinis.

Recommended spirits and champagne:
Finlandia vodka
Korbel Natural 2001 (Russian River, Sonoma, California, USA)

Caviar Canapés

4 slices white bread, crusts removed
¼ pound sweet softened butter
1 ounce wasabi tobiko caviar (flying fish roe)
4 brown organic eggs, boiled with the whites and yolks minced separately
1 teaspoon red onion, finely chopped
12 capers
1 teaspoon crème fraiche

For the toast: Cut the bread into half-inch slices to resemble ladyfingers. Be sure to remove the crusts. Toast the bread in the oven, lightly browning both sides of the bread. Set aside to cool for 5 minutes. Spread with soft butter or a compound butter of your choosing.

For the canapé: Cover one-half of the toast with caviar and the other half with two borders of minced egg. Sprinkle with a small amount of red onion. Garnish with capers. Add a small dollop of crème fraiche at each corner.

Chef's note: Never store caviar in anything that is silver or use silver spoons to serve. There are many different types of caviar on the market today. They range from the traditional caviars from Russia to salmon and lumpfish caviars from the United States. Don't be afraid to try any of these in place of the tobiko. Compound butters have had an ingredient or flavoring added to it, such as sun-dried tomatoes or chives. They can be purchased in fine food shops or you can make your own by whipping unsalted butter and then adding the desired ingredient. Spoon the softened whipped butter onto wax paper. Wrap the butter in the form of a log shape. Place in the refrigerator to harden for later use.

Chipolata

2 shallots
2 cipollini onions
2 red onions
2 Vidalia onions
3 fresh sage sprigs
6 ounces calamari, diced
2 whole garlic cloves
4 ounces pancetta, diced
1 ounce chicken livers
1½ cup Parmigiano-Reggiano cheese, grated
3 ounces soppressata
½ cup red wine
1 cup Filippo Berio olive oil
1 cup tomatoes, diced
1 French baguette
½-pound unsalted butter or margarine
1 bunch fresh chives, finely minced
¼ cup kosher salt
1 teaspoon cracked black pepper

For the chipolata: In a cast-iron skillet, add the oil until it smokes. Working quickly, add all the onions. Sauté the garlic for a few seconds or until lightly brown. Add the pancetta, cooking until golden brown. Add the meats and seafood together. Deglaze with the red wine. Reduce by half. Continue to simmer, adding the fresh sage. After about 10 minutes, it's on the way to perfection. Add the diced tomatoes. Remove the pan from the stove. Add the grated cheese, working it into the chipolata.

For the compound butter: Leave the butter out in room temperature until warm and soft to the touch but not melting. This is probably the most important part of this recipe. With a rubber-wired whisk, fold in the chives, black pepper and salt until well blended. Put in the refrigerator to set up for 2 hours. Slice the baguette into paper-thin rounds — a half-dollar shape. Spread the compound margarine on the bread. Bake the bread in a 350 degree oven for 10 minutes or until golden brown.

For the dish: Spoon the chipolata on top and enjoy. The chipolata is best when eaten warm. Garnish with a little whole chervil.

Tomato Caponata

8 Roma tomatoes, seeded and finely diced
½ eggplant, skinned and diced
½ cup shallots, diced
½ cup chives, diced
1 cup vinegar
½ cup white wine
½ cup sugar
1 tablespoon red wine vinegar
2 tablespoons capers
¼ cup black olives, diced
6 ounces Filippo Berio olive oil
2 tablespoons tomato paste
salt and pepper

For the eggplant: In a large cast-iron skillet, heat the oil to caramelize the shallots. Add the olives and the eggplant. Sauté until the eggplant is soft. Lower the heat to a simmer. Deglaze with wine. Reduce for 3 minutes. Add the tomatoes, paste, vinegars, capers, chives, salt, pepper and sugar. Bring the mixture to a steady simmer for 20 minutes. Make sure that you do not stir the mixture after this point. When it has cooled, scoop with a ladle to avoid crushing the cubed eggplant. The caponata can be used in a variety of ways: as a hors d'oeuvre, as a garnish for pasta or anything else you can think of.

Yields 1 quart.

Italian Sushi

4 large calamari, tubes only, cleaned, tentacles removed and saved for other use
2 tablespoons Filippo Berio olive oil
4 sheets nori (dried seaweed)
2 cups cooked Arborio rice, plain
½-pound black squid ink linguini
balsamic vinegar reduction in a squirt bottle (25-year-old balsamic, optional)
sun-dried tomato pesto
saffron pesto
1 zucchini, skin only and julienned
1 yellow squash, skin only and julienned
salt and pepper to taste
sweet pea (see recipe below)
sun-dried tomato pesto (see recipe below)
breadsticks for garnish

For the calamari: Marinate the calamari tubes in olive oil with salt and pepper for 1 hour. Place a sheet of nori on a clean work surface. Split the cooked Arborio rice or risotto evenly between three separate bowls. Add the sun-dried tomato pesto to the first bowl, basil pesto to the second and saffron pesto to the third. Mix each one separately with a wooden spoon, being carefully not to upset the risotto's structure. In three separate lines — but right next to each other — spread each risotto from one side of the nori to the other. Make the rice layers as thin as possible. Place an even amount of zucchini and yellow squash on the rice. Roll the nori as tight as you can — the same way you would roll sushi. Cut the nori into pieces long enough to fit inside the calamari tubes. Secure the calamari's open end with a thin wooden skewer. Place the calamari on a hot grill. Turn the tubes to put grill marks evenly on them. Place the stuffed calamari in an oven preheated to 350 degrees for 10 minutes. Remove the calamari tubes from the oven, and while still hot, slice them into rounds like sushi. Follow the plating instructions below.

For the sweet pea wasabi: In a bowl, bloom ⅛ teaspoon of wasabi paste. Place 1 cup of peas (cooked or frozen) in a blender until fully pureed. Fold in the wasabi.

For the sun-dried tomato pesto: Soak 1 cup of sun-dried tomatoes in cold water for 24 hours. Strain them. In a blender, combine the sun-dried tomatoes and ¼ cup of Filippo Berio olive oil. It will form a paste.

For the pasta: In a pasta pot, bring salted water to a boil. Add the squid ink linguini. Cook for 9 minutes, strain and then shock in cold water. Transfer the linguini to a bowl. Add the balsamic reduction with a pinch of salt. Mix well.

For the plate: Twist a handful of linguine into a neat mound in a decorative plate's center. Lay the sliced calamari around the mound. Garnish with a quenelle of sun-dried tomato pesto and a quenelle of sweet pea wasabi. In an artistic way, use the squirt bottle to apply the balsamic reduction to the dish. Garnish with thin breadsticks to resemble chopsticks.

Recommended wines:
Arancio Grillo White (Sicily, Italy)
Donna Fugata Chiaranda 2002 White (Sicily, Italy)

Parmigiano-Reggiano Crisps with Impastata and Goat Cheese

1 cup Parmigiano-Reggiano cheese, finely grated
4 ounces goat cheese
1 fresh thyme sprig, leaves removed and minced
3 ounces impastata cheese
1 teaspoon chives, minced

For the cheese crisps: Lay down a silicone baking sheet on a sheet pan, put 1 tablespoon of grated cheese in a 2-inch circle and then flatten the cheese so that it's even. Bake in a 350 degree oven until light brown. Remove from the oven. Place several small ramekins upside down on a flat surface. With a spatula, remove the cheese and then put it on top of the ramekin. Flatten it out and around to form a cup.

For the mousse: In a stand mixer, add the goat cheese and the impastata. Mix until blended. Stop the mixer to fold in the chives by hand. Pipe it into the cheese cup using a pastry bag. Assemble like an artist!

Recommended wines:
Late Harvest Riesling Jekel 2001 (Monterey County, California, USA)
Fetzer Echo Ridge Sauvignon Blanc 2003 (Mendocino County, California, USA)

Prosciutto and Fig Canapés

4 slices prosciutto di Parma
1 pint black mission figs
8 ounces mascarpone cheese, at room temperature
1 fresh mint sprig for garnish

For the canapé: This is a very easy classic; it's waiting for you on a delightful summer day in the shade. Wash the black mission figs. Immediately dry the figs on paper, toweling quickly. Refrigerate for 2 hours. I find that this brings the taste alive again. Slice the prosciutto paper-thin. Layer it on wax paper, stacking each sheet overlapping the next to avoid drying out. Wrap a slice of prosciutto di Parma once around a mission fig, exposing the stem. Slice a piece from the bottom so that it will sit upright on the plate without falling over. Put a dollop of mascarpone cheese on top. Garnish with a mint leaf. Simple perfection!

Recommended drink:
Sparkling Freixenet Corta Nevada Secco (Spain)

Tomato and Anchovy Canapés

3 garlic cloves, roasted
1 teaspoon crème fraiche
10 anchovy fillets, mashed
1 tablespoon red onion, minced
4 heirloom tomatoes, peeled, seeded and chopped
1 fresh chives sprig
12 black Kalamata olives, pitted and cut in half
12 sun-dried tomatoes
4 teaspoons Filippo Berio olive oil
¼ pound unsalted butter, softened
salt and pepper to taste
10 slices white bread with the crust removed

For the tomato and anchovy paste: In a blender, puree half the anchovies with the roasted garlic. In a pan on high heat, add the oil to brown the onions. Add the anchovy mixture to the pan. Stir together for 1 minute. Add the sun-dried and fresh heirloom tomatoes to the pan. Continue to cook for 7 minutes — until it starts to reduce. Do not stop cooking until the mixture looks like it has lost most of its natural juices.

For the toast: Cut the bread into half-inch slices to resemble ladyfingers. Be sure to remove the crusts. Toast bread in the oven, lightly browning both sides. Set to cool for 5 minutes. Spread with soft butter or a compound butter.

For the assembly: Spread some tomato-anchovy paste on the toast. Garnish with the remaining anchovies, putting a dollop of crème fraiche on top. Garnish with the halved olives. Sprinkle salt and pepper to taste. Alternatively, add some diced chives on top of the crème fraiche.

Chef's note: Keep in mind that olives and anchovies are generally salty. Measure your desired taste.

Recommended drinks:
Pedro Domecq Amontillado sherry (Jerez, Spain)
Quinta Do Noval 10-year-old Tawny port (Portugal)

Roasted Fingerling Potatoes with Crème Fraiche and Caviar

4 pounds unpeeled fingerling potatoes, such as Russian Banana
4 tablespoons Filippo Berio olive oil
1 tablespoon rosemary, minced
1 tablespoon flat-leaf parsley, minced
1 tablespoon fresh thyme, stems removed and leaves finely chopped
2 cups crème fraiche or sour cream
black caviar
kosher salt and black pepper to taste

For the potatoes: Clean and slice the potatoes lengthwise. Place them in a large bowl. Add the olive oil, rosemary, parsley, salt and pepper. Toss well. Arrange the potatoes cut-side down on lightly greased baking sheets. Roast in a preheated 400 degree oven until the potatoes are brown, crisp and cooked through. Allow them to slightly cool.

For the table: Arrange the potatoes on platters cut-side up. Place the caviar and crème fraiche in bowls next to the platters.

Chef's note: High-quality imported caviar can be very expensive. Try domestic lumpfish or paddlefish roe or flying fish roe. The potatoes can also be used as a passed hors d'oeuvre. Spoon crème fraiche and caviar on each potato. Arrange them on passing trays.

There are quite an immense variety of soups, which could lead to confusion. Soups can be divided into bisques, bouillons, consommés, purees and minestrones.

Usually, soups such as the bouillons might be garnished with either pasta or rice. They also tend to have cubes of vegetables and meats floating throughout the soup. Bouillons are the basis of various consommés — each distinctive from the rest.

Consommés are served in tea cups, accompanied by mild-strength grated cheese. The cheese should never overpower the soup's flavor or hide the natural flavorings in any way. There are also soups called "double consommés," which are usually served at elaborate dinner parties.

Purees — otherwise known as a "potage" — are made with a single puree or a mixture of purees. They are served with garnishes, such as baby lentils, boiled potatoes or large poached vegetables. I like to refer to puree soups as the "hungry man's special."

Bisques are almost always referred to as thick soups based on shellfish. Cream and roux are added to these soups to help with the thickening process.

Classic soups compiled in the warm country of Italy, minestrone soups are distinguished for their presence of beautifully flavored vegetables. A bowl of this soup with a piece of bread will send you sleeping for hours. Good minestrone will have the taste of the garden, with the vegetables retaining their shapes.

Soups

Crayfish Bisque

3 pounds crayfish, cleaned thoroughly in running cold water
2 cups dry red wine
4 quarts seafood bouillon or fish stock
½ cup butter
1 cup Filippo Berio olive oil
2 large carrots, diced
2 large onions, diced
1 small celery stalk, diced
1 bunch fresh thyme, leaves pulled and stems discarded
5 tablespoons brandy
2 bay leaves
2 Italian flat-leaf parsley sprigs
5 cups heavy cream
1 16-ounce can plum tomatoes
2 tablespoons Renaissance Farms garlic salt
¼ teaspoon white pepper
¼ teaspoon black pepper
1 cup cooked rice

For the bisque: In a large, heavy saucepot on high heat, add oil and butter. Immediately add the carrots, celery, onions, cooked rice and fresh thyme. Cook until brown and well caramelized. Add the crayfish. Continue to sauté for about 4 minutes. Cover the pot with a lid. When the crayfish start to turn a bright red color, deglaze with red wine and brandy. Cook down until half evaporates. Add the heavy cream and the seafood bouillon. Bring the mixture to a simmer. Add the bay leaf and black and white pepper. Continue to cook for another 30 minutes. Smash the crayfish, breaking the shells. This technique will allow you to maximize the seafood's flavor. Return the cracked crayfish to the pot. Cook for another 5 minutes. Strain twice through a China cap. Set aside.
For the froth: In a blender, turn on the lowest speed while it's empty. Carefully add the hot bisque to the blender — 3 ounces at a time. Add the rice. Blend until smooth. Eventually, add the remaining bisque, blending on high until smooth. Adjust the seasoning to taste.
For the plate: Place the fried basil and 1 teaspoon of crème fraiche in the soup's middle.

Serves 10.

Recommended wines:
Jade Mountain Syrah 2000 (Napa Valley, California, USA)
Qupe Syrah 2002 (Santa Monica, California, USA)

Golden Gazpacho

2 pounds yellow tomatoes, seeds removed and diced
1 pound yellow pepper, diced small
10 ounces cucumber, peeled, seeded and diced
10 ounces yellow squash, seeded and diced
1 ounce garlic, minced
2 ounces white wine vinegar
2 ounces lemon juice
1 ounce Filippo Berio olive oil
hot pepper sauce, to taste
salt and pepper, to taste
1 quart vegetable stock
8 ounces jumbo lump crabmeat
2 ounces radish shoots

For the soup: Except for the vegetable stock, hot pepper sauce, salt, pepper and crabmeat, place all ingredients into a food processor. Pulse only — do not puree, as the soup should have visible pieces from each vegetable. Remove from the food processor and then place in a large bowl. Add the stock so that the consistency is thinner. Add stock as needed. Adjust the seasoning with salt, pepper and hot sauce to taste. Chill well until ready to serve.

For the plate: Pour the gazpacho into 8 soup bowls. In the bowl's center, place approximately 1 ounce of crabmeat into the gazpacho. Top the gazpacho with radish shoots. Serve well chilled.

Serves 8.

Rice and Sausage Soup

4 tablespoons Filippo Berio olive oil
1 tablespoon duck fat (optional)
½ pound very lean ground pork
3 shallots, diced
3 celery stalks, diced
1 bunch fresh thyme, tied
3 quarts chicken stock
1 turnip, diced
¼ pound prosciutto, diced
1 bunch Italian flat-leaf parsley, tied
3 garlic cloves
2 whole carrots, peeled and diced
salt and black pepper to taste
1½ cups Parmigiano-Reggiano cheese, freshly grated
1 cup uncooked rice
sun-dried tomatoes (optional)

For the soup: In a large pot on high heat, add the oil and the duck fat until very hot. Add the diced shallots, garlic, carrots, celery, prosciutto and fresh thyme. Sweat them until they caramelize. Add the chicken stock and the parsley with the salt and pepper. Bring to a boil. Add the pork, diced turnips and the rice. Lower to a simmer. Cook until the rice is al dente — usually between 16 to 19 minutes. At this point, you can skim the oil from the soup's surface. However, some fat should be left, as it adds to the dish's flavor.

For the dish: Add the cheese, stirring it into the soup. Crack fresh black pepper to float on the top. Some grilled peasant bread really goes well with this dish.

For the garnish: I like something that is acidic so that it cuts through some of the soup's fat. Sun-dried tomatoes work well. Alternatively, try oven-drying your own tomatoes. Slice some tomatoes to place in an oven at 150 degrees for 8 hours. When the moisture is totally gone from the tomatoes, take them from the oven. Lay the tomato slices on top of the soup.

Serves 8.

Oyster Stew

6 tablespoons Filippo Berio olive oil
4 potatoes, peeled and diced
3 shallot bulbs, peeled and diced
3 celery stalks, diced
½ onion, peeled and diced
2 carrots, diced
1 quart water
½ gallon freshly shucked oysters in liquor
1 teaspoon nutmeg
1 cup Chardonnay
1 pint heavy cream
6 tablespoons flour
½ bunch fresh thyme, leaves pulled off
salt and white pepper to taste

For the stew: In a large saucepan on high heat, add the oil. When the oil becomes hot, add the diced shallots and onion. Cook until translucent. Add the carrot and celery. Cook 5 to 7 minutes more. Sift the flour into the saucepan, stirring it into the vegetables. Deglaze with Chardonnay, adding the cream, water and potatoes. Bring to a boil. Lower to a simmer and reduce. When the potatoes are fork-tender, add the oysters. Bring the stew back to a boil. Reduce until nappe (when liquid sheets or coats a spoon's back). Season with salt, pepper and fresh thyme.

For the dish: Spoon the stew into rustic bowls. Serve with a warm, buttered sourdough roll.

For the garnish: Something spicy is needed. Roll 1 oyster in a mixture of cornmeal, salt, pepper and cayenne. Flash fry and then float in the bowl's middle. Or try a drizzle of a flavorful hot sauce — but not too much. We don't want to take away from the stew's flavor.

Serves 6.

Saffron Oyster Stew

48 shucked oysters, Blue Point (or another Atlantic oyster) whole and liquid reserved
½-pound apple-smoked bacon (like Nueske's), cut into small pieces
1 cup clam juice
¼ cup flour
1 quart heavy cream
12 saffron threads
2 tablespoons unsalted butter
1 shallot, finely chopped
1 small onion, coarsely chopped
3 Yukon Gold potatoes, cut into cubes
¼ cup dry white wine
salt and pepper to taste

For the stew: Melt butter in a heavy saucepan. Add the bacon, cooking until it starts to brown. With a slotted spoon, remove and discard as much bacon as you can. Add the shallot and onion. Sauté until wilted, but do not brown. Add the flour, stirring it into the onions. Deglaze with the white wine, adding the clam juice and reserved oyster juice. Add the potatoes and saffron. Stir to mix. Add the heavy cream. Cook on a low heat until the potatoes are soft but not falling apart. Stir to prevent sticking.

For the plate: Add the oysters to the stew. Cook until the oysters start to curl. Do not overcook the oysters or they will be tough. Adjust the seasoning with salt and pepper. Remove the oysters from the heat. Ladle them into bowls. Before serving, drizzle white truffle oil around each bowl. Serve with crusty bread.

Recommended drink:

Open House Punch:

1/5 Southern Comfort
6 ounces lemon juice
6 ounces frozen lemonade
6 ounces frozen orange juice
3 liters 7-UP

In a bowl, mix the punch with orange and lemon wedges.

Chinese Cabbage and Lobster Soup

For the consommé:
2 celery stalks
2 carrots, peeled and diced
2 garlic cloves, roasted
1 fresh thyme sprig
1 leek, cleaned and diced
1 shallot
1 2½-pound lobster

For the soup:
1 shallot, diced
½ cup carrots, diced
½ cup celery, diced
1 small Chinese cabbage, cut into quarters and core removed
¼ cup radicchio
¼ cup fresh baby spinach
2 tablespoons Filippo Berio olive oil
3 tablespoons crème fraiche
salt and cracked pepper to taste

For the lobster consommé: Bring 2½ quarts of water to a boil in a heavy pot. Add the celery, carrots, garlic, shallots, leeks and thyme. Add the lobster, making sure that it's totally submerged in the water. Cook for 15 minutes. Remove the lobster and then place it in the refrigerator for later use. Strain the liquid through a cheesecloth. Reserve it for the next step. When it has cooled, remove all the meat from the lobster's shell. Be sure not to smash the meat when cracking the shell.

For the soup: In a large pot, add the olive oil, heating until it starts to smoke. Add the shallots, carrots and celery. Sweat them for 4 minutes or until slightly brown. Add the cabbage, baby spinach and radicchio. Cook until wilted but not brown. Pour the lobster consommé into the pot. Boil it for 15 minutes or until the cabbage is completely soft.

For the plate: Pour 8 ounces of the soup into a bowl. Add lobster meat. Garnish with a teaspoon of crème fraiche.

Serves 6.

Sweet Potato Vichyssoise

2 pounds sweet potatoes, peeled and diced
1 bunch leeks, whites only, cleaned well and chopped
½ stick unsalted butter
1 small onion, diced small
1 pint heavy cream
1 quart chicken stock
1 bay leaf
1 fresh thyme sprig
¼ teaspoon ground nutmeg
8 ounces cooked lobster meat, tail and claws
1 package daikon radish sprouts
salt and white pepper to taste

To start: In a heavy pot, melt butter to cook the leeks until soft. Do not brown. Stir in diced onions, followed by the addition of sweet potatoes and chicken stock. Add the bay leaf and thyme. Bring to a boil. Reduce the heat to simmer. Season the mixture with nutmeg, salt and white pepper. Remove the pot from the heat when the potatoes are soft. Strain and reserve the liquid from the vegetables. Place the vegetables in a food processor. Blend well. Slowly add the strained liquid to the processor, but do not use all the liquid. Reserve any extra liquid to thin out the soup if it becomes too thick. Remove blended ingredients from processor. Return the pot to the stove. Add the heavy cream by whisking it in. Turn the heat up to medium. Remove the pot when the soup comes to a boil. Chill the soup before serving.

For the plate: Adjust the seasoning before plating. Pour the soup into bowls. Garnish with lobster meat and daikon sprouts. Serve well chilled.

Serves 4 to 6.

Seafood Cappuccino

Soup:
2 white onions, diced
2 large carrots, diced
½ bunch Italian flat-leaf parsley, chopped
2 small shallots, finely diced
2 pounds shellfish shells, including shrimp and lobster bodies (ask your fishmonger what he or she has available)
1 pint heavy cream
1 thyme sprig, leaves removed and diced
1 cup garlic, thinly sliced
1 pound butter
¼ cup Filippo Berio olive oil
2 quarts fresh clam juice
1 pound lobster meat
1 pound bacon, diced
salt and pepper to taste

Roux:
4 tablespoons butter (half a stick)
½ cup flour
Make a ¼ pound blond roux (you will only use half of that)

Cappuccino:
1½ quarts (6 cups) heavy cream

For the soup: In a heavy-bottom stockpot, add the 1 pound of butter and olive oil. Melt on high heat. Add all the vegetables, seasonings and bacon. Sauté until golden brown and most of the bacon fat is rendered. Add the pint of heavy cream and clam juice to the pot — except for the lobster and the roux. Cook down until one-third reduced. Strain through cheesecloth. Follow the instructions below for adding the roux and finishing the soup.

For the roux: Melt butter in a heavy pan over low heat. Stir in the flour. Cook until the mixture is the consistency of wet sand and has a toasted aroma. Do not brown the roux. When the roux is done, add 2 cups of soup broth to the pan — a little at a time — whisking to create a smooth mixture. Add more soup to thin out the mixture. When you are sure there are no lumps, add the entire mixture to the soup. Bring to a boil. Reduce the heat. Whisk until smooth and well blended.

For the cappuccino: In a blender, add 1 cup of heavy cream. Whip it until it turns to cream. For each serving: In a blender, combine 8 ounces of the thickened soup with 2 ounces of lobster meat until the mixture is creamy and frothy. When adding a hot substance, be sure to always have the blender running, pouring in the soup a little at a time. Repeat this process until you have the desired amount of servings. Garnish the cappuccino with lobster meat or crabmeat.

For the plate: Garnish the cappuccino with the remaining lobster pieces.

Serves 6.

Recommended wines:
St. Suprey Sauvignon Blanc 2002 (Napa, California, USA)
Cosentino "The Novelist" 2000 (Napa, California, USA)

Chef

Lentil Soup with Smoked Ham

1½ tablespoons Filippo Berio olive oil
1½ cups smoked ham, diced
1 small onion, finely diced
1½ teaspoons dry mustard
3 cups chicken stock
1 cup mixed lentils
3 garlic cloves, roasted
1 pound tomatoes, diced
salt and pepper to taste

For the soup: Heat the oil in a large saucepan over medium heat. Add the ham and the mustard. Cook until the ham begins to brown. Add the diced onion. Sauté until soft. Add the roasted garlic. Stir. Add the lentils and the tomatoes. Mix well. Add the stock. Simmer uncovered for 20 minutes until the lentils are tender. Add additional stock to thin the soup if desired. Adjust the seasoning with salt and pepper.

Serves 2.

Beef Barley Soup

3 pounds beef shoulder, cut into cubes
2 tablespoons Filippo Berio olive oil
8 cups beef stock
4 ounces tomato paste
1 cup celery, diced
3 carrots, peeled and chopped
1 large onion, chopped
½ cup pearl barley, well rinsed
6 large garlic cloves, chopped
3 bay leaves
6 ounces mushrooms, sliced
kosher salt and pepper to taste

For the soup: In a large skillet, heat the oil over medium heat until hot. Add the beef. Brown it well. Drain the fat from the beef. In a large stockpot, add the drained beef and all the other ingredients. Bring the mixture to a boil. Reduce to a simmer for 1 hour. Stir occasionally. When the beef is very tender and shredding, remove it from heat. Serve it in large bowls.

Serves 6 to 8.

There are a variety of lettuces and vegetables that appear in markets when they are in season. I strongly recommend that the following recipes be made with only the freshest vegetables for the best results. All greens should be crisp, with color being the number one standard for purchasing. When shopping for the best produce, try and purchase locally grown produce. It will be far superior in taste and texture than that which has been shipped from all parts of the states. There are many well-known and respected companies that specialize in this service. However, for the average shopper, I recommend the suggestions above.

Salads

Warm Lobster Salad with Peaches

I think that lobsters and peaches are such a natural together that I have included two different garnishes for this colorful lobster salad. Enjoy either one!

1 pound lobster meat, cooked, chilled and shelled
3 ounces bacon, diced
3 garlic cloves
1 pint small pear-shaped tomatoes, yellow and red
1 red onion, thinly sliced
½ cup rosemary, chopped
½ cup basil, chopped
1 loaf focaccia bread
1 tablespoon Filippo Berio olive oil
½ cup grape seed oil
¼ cup shredded Asiago cheese
2 cups carrots, shredded
2 peaches, pits removed and quartered
½ cup peach liqueur
1 flat or donut peach, seeded and quartered
1 cup aged balsamic vinegar
salt and pepper to taste
4 ounces mesclun greens
2 pieces hearts of palm, quartered and julienned
1 head baby frisée lettuce
1 Belgian endive bulb
1 head baby radicchio
peaches, poached in red wine
¼ cup tangerine juice
2 ounces cracked Calabrese olives
3 ounces goat cheese

For the dressing: Add oil, garlic and basil to the hot pan. Be careful, as the basil will splatter. Add the bacon. Continue to brown. Take the pan off the heat. Deglaze with peach liqueur. Add the peaches and tangerine juice. Return the pan to the heat. Continue to reduce by half. Add the cooked lobster and pear-shaped tomatoes, toss to coat and remove them from heat.

For the salad: In a bowl, add the mesclun greens, frisée, sliced endive, radicchio, carrots and hearts of palm. Fluff up the salad with your hands to ensure that all the vegetables are properly mixed before adding the vinegar. Add the warm dressing into the salad, mixing it very carefully. Add a tablespoon of Filippo Berio olive oil.

For the focaccia: If using focaccia as a garnish, slice the focaccia bread. Toast it lightly on both sides until golden brown. When the bread has cooled, spread some goat cheese on top.

For the plate: Place the dressed greens in the center of individual plates. Carefully place the lobster on top of the greens. Garnish the salad with the focaccia and goat cheese. Garnish with cracked Calabrese olives and shredded Asiago cheese.

Recommended wines:
Moreau & Fils Chablis 2002 (Chablis, France)
Mommessin Pouilly-Fuissé 2003

IMPORTED FROM ITALY
100% PURE ALL NATURAL
FILIPPO BERIO
OLIVE OIL
SUPERB ORIGINAL FLAVOR
CHOLESTEROL INFORMATION ON BACK PANEL
NET 25.5 FL OZ (1 PT 9.5 FL OZ) - 750 ml

Salad of Baby Field Greens with Oven-Roasted Tomatoes and Port Wine Vinaigrette

For the dried tomatoes:
6 whole plum tomatoes, cut in half lengthwise
1 teaspoon fresh thyme, minced and without stems
¼ cup Filippo Berio olive oil
fine sea salt to taste · 1 shallot, minced

For the port wine vinaigrette:
1 gallon port wine · 1 quart cranberry juice
6 ounces blackberry jam
1 cucumber, peeled and diced
1 pint grape seed oil, in a squirt bottle
1 teaspoon kosher salt

For the salad (per serving):
1 ounce mesclun greens · 1 ounce micro greens
½ ounce pea tendrils · ½ ounce mache lettuce
1 tablespoon Gorgonzola cheese
1 ounce pancetta, cooked and diced
1 Bartlett pear, skinned and diced for garnish

For the tomatoes: Place the halved tomatoes in a stainless steel bowl. Add the thyme, sea salt, oil and shallot. Mix gently, being sure not to upset the tomato's shape. Lay the tomatoes cut-side down on a rack set over a baking sheet. Leave them in a 150 degree oven for 12 hours.

For the dressing: In a heavy-bottom pot, reduce the port wine by one-third. Add the cranberry to the port. Reduce by half. Stir in the jam while on low simmer. Reduce until the liquid coats a spoon's back. Add the teaspoons of salt at the very end.

For the plate: Put all the greens in a stainless steel bowl, adding 2 tablespoons of port wine vinaigrette and 2 tablespoons of grape seed oil. Add a pinch of fine sea salt. Mix gently. Form the sliced cucumber into a ring, filling the center with lettuce. Add the pancetta and the Gorgonzola cheese on the top and the roasted tomatoes to the side of it.

Chef's note: Put the remainder of port wine and the oil in a squeeze bottle for future use. The greens will only yield 1 order. Happy eating!

Serves 4.

Recommended wines:
Quinta Do Noval 20-year-old Tawny port (Portugal)
Cockburns Late Bottle Vintage 1997 (Portugal)

Crab and Walnuts with Creamsicle Vinaigrette

3 ounces Phillips lump crabmeat
8 orange segments
½ pint yellow cherry tomatoes, cut in half
½ pint red cherry tomatoes, cut in half
1 Belgian endive, leaves separated
1 red radish, thinly sliced
½ avocado, diced
1 tablespoon grape seed oil
½ cup tangerine juice
½ cup coconut milk
1 tablespoon walnuts, coarsely chopped
5 baby spinach leaves, cut into a chiffonade
salt and pepper to taste

For the vinaigrette: In a blender, add the tangerine juice and coconut milk. Pulse for 10 seconds. Gradually add the oil while the blender is on high to emulsify the mixture. The vinaigrette will thicken slightly. Reserve it for later use.

For the salad: In a stainless steel bowl, add the crabmeat, orange segments, sliced radish, walnuts, avocado and spinach. Add 3 tablespoons of vinaigrette. Toss gently. Add salt and pepper to taste.

For the plate: On a 10½-inch plate, spread the endive in the plate's center. Form a ring mold of crab salad directly on the endive. Place the cherry tomatoes around the mold. Spoon some vinaigrette around the mold for garnish.

Recommended wines:
Floral Springs Sangiovese 2002 Red (Napa Valley, California, USA)
Geyser Peak Viognier Preston Vineyard White (Dry Creek Valley, Sonoma, California, USA)

Serves 3.

The Leaning Salad of Pisa

½ cup red wine vinegar
2 cups orange juice
1 cup port wine reduction
7 gelatin sheets, bloomed in cold water
12 ounces yellow beet juice
12 ounces red beet juice
1 cup grape seed oil
3 cups mixed baby greens
1 cup baby frisée lettuce
pinch granulated sugar
2 tablespoons grape seed oil
1 tablespoon flowering herbs (optional)
4 tangerines, segmented
3 ounces Gorgonzola cheese, cut into 1-inch dice
kosher salt and pepper to taste

For the dressing: In a plastic spray bottle, add the grape seed oil, red wine vinegar and orange juice. Shake well. Leave in the refrigerator until ready to serve.

For the salad: In a stainless steel bowl, combine all the greens. Lightly coat them with 2 teaspoons of grape seed oil. Salt and pepper to taste. Add the chopped basil, tangerines and flowering herbs. Set aside.

For the gelée: In a saucepan, heat up the beet juice in separate pots. Bring the juice to a boil. Add a pinch of salt and granulated sugar until the desired taste is created. Shut the heat off. Stir in half the bloomed gelatin sheets into each juice until completely dissolved. Pour the yellow and red beet gelatin in separate 2-inch terrine molds. Refrigerate until it's set and firm (usually 3 hours).

For the plate: In a large, 12-inch, flat plate, build your salad to resemble a tall tower in the center. Slowly building the frisée will help with the height. Place the Gorgonzola pieces around the salad. This will help with creating the structure. Cut the gelatin into half-inch squares. Place them against the salad. Finally, spray the bottle of dressing twice on the greens at the mist level.

Serves 3.

The Little Pepper from Spain

6 medium-sized piquillo peppers
3 ounces Boursin cheese, at room temperature
1 bunch chives, minced
1 tomato, blanched, peeled and seeded
3 garlic cloves, roasted and cooled
6 ounces fennel, sliced paper-thin
1 cup orange juice
1 orange, segmented and rind removed
½ cup cooked white beans, pureed with 1 roasted garlic clove
red pepper reduction for garnish

For the fennel: On a slicing machine or mandoline, shave thin slices of fennel into a bowl. Add orange juice and chives. Marinate for 24 hours. The fennel will absorb the taste of the orange juice and release its natural flavor.

For the plate: Fill the piquillo peppers with Boursin cheese. Work carefully, as the piquillo peppers are fragile. If you prefer, use a pastry bag to pipe the cheese directly into the peppers. Place a stuffed piquillo pepper in the plate's center. Next to the pepper, place 1 ounce of fennel right up against it. Place the orange segment next to the fennel. Spoon a little bean puree on the other side of the pepper. Cut the tomato into wedges. Place a wedge in the bean puree. Finally, add some red pepper reduction to the plate for added pepper flavor.

Chef's note: Piquillo peppers come from the Ebro River Valley in northern Spain. They are slow-roasted over wood fires that concentrate their intense flavor. Red or ripe piquillos are the most common seen, although green or unripe peppers are starting to appear in the market. In the United States, piquillo peppers are never seen fresh, only in jars. If you are unable to find piquillos, substitute any small pepper.

Makes 6 peppers to serve 3.

Couscous Salad with Walnuts and Dates

1 box Mediterranean-style couscous
1 teaspoon salt
2 cups boiling water
¼ cup lemon juice
½ cup Filippo Berio olive oil
¼ tablespoon lime zest
¼ tablespoon lemon zest
1 fresh mint sprig, diced
½ teaspoon chives, minced
¼ cup feta cheese, crumbled
8 ounces garbanzo beans (I recommend cooking them from the dry state)
⅔ cup pitted dates, diced
½ cup walnuts, chopped
1 plum tomato, seeded and minced

For the couscous: In a large stainless steel bowl, add the couscous, salt and boiling water. Cover the bowl completely with plastic wrap to allow the couscous to steam. Set aside.

For the walnut and date vinaigrette: Whisk the olive oil, lemon juice, lemon zest and lime zest until mixed. Mix in the garbanzo beans, dates, feta cheese, chives and mint. Whisk vigorously to incorporate all ingredients. Add the tomato and walnuts at the very end. Set aside.

For the plate: Remove the plastic from the bowl. With a fork, fluff the couscous until the grains are not sticking together. Pour the vinaigrette over the couscous, mixing it well.

Chef's note: When you place the couscous back in the refrigerator for more than 2 hours, it will absorb all the oil. You can easily add more oil to loosen it back up when you are ready to eat it again.

Serves 4.

Salad of Fennel, Radicchio and Endive

1 head fennel, tops removed
2 heads radicchio
2 heads endive
1 shallot, minced
½ cup Filippo Berio olive oil
½ cup raspberry vinegar
salt and pepper to taste

For the salad: Remove the tops from the fennel, saving them for the garnish. Cut the bulb in half. With a sharp knife, carefully shave thin slices off. As an alternative, use a mandoline to achieve very thin shavings. Remove the larger outer leaves from the radicchio. Save them to form a cup. Shave the radicchio as thin as possible. A mandoline is also perfect for this task. Do the same with the endive. Mix all shaved vegetables together in a bowl. Set aside.

For the dressing: Preheat a small sauté pan with a little olive oil. When hot, add the minced shallots. Brown them well, but do not burn. Remove the pan from the heat to allow the shallots to slightly cool. Pour in the raspberry vinegar. Mix well. Allow to cool further. Pour the dressing into a mixing bowl. Whisk in the olive oil. Season with salt and pepper. Pour the dressing over the shaved vegetables. Mix well.

For the plate: Form a cup with several saved radicchio leaves. Place it in a salad plate's center. Fill the cup with the salad. Repeat to make 6 salads. Break off pieces from the fennel top. Creatively place them on the salad. Drizzle a little raspberry vinegar on the plate before serving.

Serves 6.

SHRIMP
CALAMARI
CALAMARI
Cocktail
Claws
2 lb. Bag
$31.90
King
Crab

Pistachio Watercress Salad

4 brown organic eggs
1 cup milk
1 cup plus 3 tablespoons flour, sifted
6 tablespoons melted butter
Filippo Berio olive oil as needed
1 bunch washed watercress
1 tablespoon pistachio nuts
1 large yellow tomato, seeded and quartered
½-pound pancetta, diced
Grand Cru Gruyère cheese (optional)

Special equipment: A 12-inch nonstick pan will be needed for making the crepe.

For the crepe: In a large stainless steel bowl, beat the eggs. While whisking the eggs, slowly add the milk. Add the flour and the melted butter, constantly whipping. When the batter is smooth and free from any lumps, the mixture is finished. I like to place the batter in the refrigerator for at least 2 hours. This gives the flour a chance to absorb the eggs. The batter should not be as thick as pancake batter. If it is, just add cold water or milk to bring it back. Place a 12-inch nonstick pan over medium heat. The best way to grease the pan is to work some butter into a clean rag's tip. The butter should be room temperature. Rub the rag's tip in the butter. Butter the pan with the rag, making sure to grease the whole inside. Place the pan back on the fire. Put a 4-ounce ladle of batter into the pan, moving the pan around to coat the bottom evenly. The crepe is ready to be turned when the edges start to pull away from the pan and curl. Remove the crepe from the pan once the other side is cooked. Continue making crepes using the remaining batter.

For the greens: In a sauté pan on medium, heat 2 tablespoons of olive oil until hot. Add the raw diced pancetta, letting it render until brown. Take the pan off the fire. Throw the watercress into the hot oil for about 3 seconds. The whole idea of this is just to wilt the greens. Put the greens into a bowl. When the oil has cooled, add it to the bowl as well. Add the pistachio nuts and tomatoes.

For the plate: In a 10-inch flat dish, place the crepe in the center. Place all the watercress and the remainder of olive oil in the center. This recipe goes real well with some shaved, hard Grand Cru Gruyère cheese.

Lobster Salad Timbale with Peaches

1 2½ to 3-pound lobster, steamed and meat removed from the shell
3 strips bacon, diced and cooked
3 garlic cloves, chopped
1 pint pear-shaped tomatoes, yellow and red
4 ounces fennel, thinly sliced
1 red onion, thinly sliced
1 bunch alfalfa sprouts
½ cup grape seed oil
2 cups shredded carrots
½ cup peach liqueur
1 cup aged balsamic vinegar
salt and pepper to taste
4 ounces watercress
1 ripe peach, thinly sliced

For the lobster: In a 3-quart pot, fill three-fourths of it with hot water. When the water starts to boil, place the lobster in it. It will take about 14 minutes to cook. Remove the lobster from the water. Take the claws and tail off from the lobster's body. Place the lobster pieces in an ice bath for 15 minutes. Crack the lobster shells, removing the meat. Slice the lobster meat very thin. Set aside for later use.

For the vinaigrette: In a stainless steel bowl, add the grape seed oil, balsamic vinegar, carrots, peach liqueur, fennel and red onion. Let those ingredients sit in the liquid for 15 minutes. The acid from the vinegar will help soften the vegetables. Whisk the ingredients in the bowl together before adding all remaining ingredients — except for the watercress and peaches. The tomatoes, bacon and lobster meat should be carefully mixed in by hand. Adjust the seasoning with salt and pepper.

For the plate: Arrange a bed of watercress on a large plate. Place the lobster mixture over the greens. Arrange peach slices around the lobster. Top the salad with any liquid from the lobster and the alfalfa sprouts. There are plenty of colors working here, so make sure that they are all visible.

Serves 4.

Crab Louis

½ cup mayonnaise
2 tablespoons chili sauce
2 tablespoon Dijon mustard
2 tablespoon fresh lemon juice
1 teaspoon lemon peel, grated
1 pound mixed field greens
2 avocados, peeled, halved and pitted
1 pound Phillips jumbo lump crabmeat
1 small bunch chives, finely minced

For the salad: Whisk the mayonnaise, chili sauce, mustard, lemon juice and lemon peel together in a small bowl. Season with salt and pepper to taste. Arrange the greens on 4 plates. Place an avocado half cut-side up on the plate. Break up the crabmeat slightly with your fingers. Divide it among the 4 plates. Spoon the dressing over the crab. Garnish with chives.

Serves 4.

Petite Heirloom Tomatoes

1 green zebra tomato
1 yellow Brandywine tomato
1 red Brandywine tomato
1 orange tomato · 1 bunch chives
1 cubinelle pepper · ½ teaspoon sea salt
1 tablespoon apple cider vinegar
1 ounce balsamic vinegar reduction or aged balsamic vinegar
½ sheet puff pastry, available frozen
3 shallots · 3 basil leaves
2 tablespoons unsalted butter
1 cup blended canola olive oil, available in most supermarkets

For the tomatoes: Place a large pot three-fourths full with cold water on high heat. Score each tomato with one cut from top to bottom. Make sure that the cut is not too deep and that it only penetrates the skin. Once the water boils, lower the temperature to a simmer. Place a dish on top of the tomatoes so that they stay submerged. Cook for 5 minutes. When the skin starts to peel away from the body, remove the tomatoes from the pot. Quickly place them in an ice bath to cool. Take the tomatoes from the ice. Dry them on a towel. Peel the skin from the tomatoes, leaving the bodies whole. Cut the tomatoes in half. Place them on a rack over a sheet pan — cut-side down — and refrigerate for a half hour. Remove the tomatoes. Slice the halves into quarters. Remove the cores. Place them in a stainless steel bowl until the vinaigrette is ready.

For the cubinelle vinaigrette: In a blender, add the diced pepper, apple cider vinegar and blended oil. Blend on high until emulsified. Strain the vinaigrette. Store it in a squeeze bottle until ready to use.

For the puff pastry: Roast the shallots in a 350 degree oven until brown. Place in a blender with butter and basil. Mix well. Strain the mixture. Cut 3-inch rounds from the puff pastry using a cookie cutter. Brush with shallot butter. Bake until golden brown.

For the plate: Place a piece of the puff pastry in the plate's center. Arrange 1 slice of each tomato around the pastry. Drizzle the vinaigrette over the tomatoes. Finish with the balsamic reduction. Garnish with fresh basil and chives.

Chef's note: Heirloom tomatoes are a summer treat. They are becoming more readily available at supermarkets but are very common at farm stands. There are many different varieties and colors. If you can't find the varieties mentioned above, use what is available in your area.

Serves 4.

Chicken Salad with Grapes and Walnuts

4 cups chicken breast meat, cooked and cubed
1 cup walnuts, toasted and chopped
½ cup celery, chopped
2 tablespoons shallots, finely chopped
1 cup red grapes, cut in half
1 cup green grapes, cut in half
1 cup mayonnaise
3 tablespoons tarragon vinegar
2 tablespoons tarragon, freshly chopped
10 ounces mixed field greens
salt and white pepper to taste

For the salad: Toss all the ingredients — except for the field greens — together in a large bowl. Combine well. Refrigerate for 1 hour before serving. Divide the field greens onto 4 plates. Place approximately 1 cup of salad on each plate.

Serves 4.

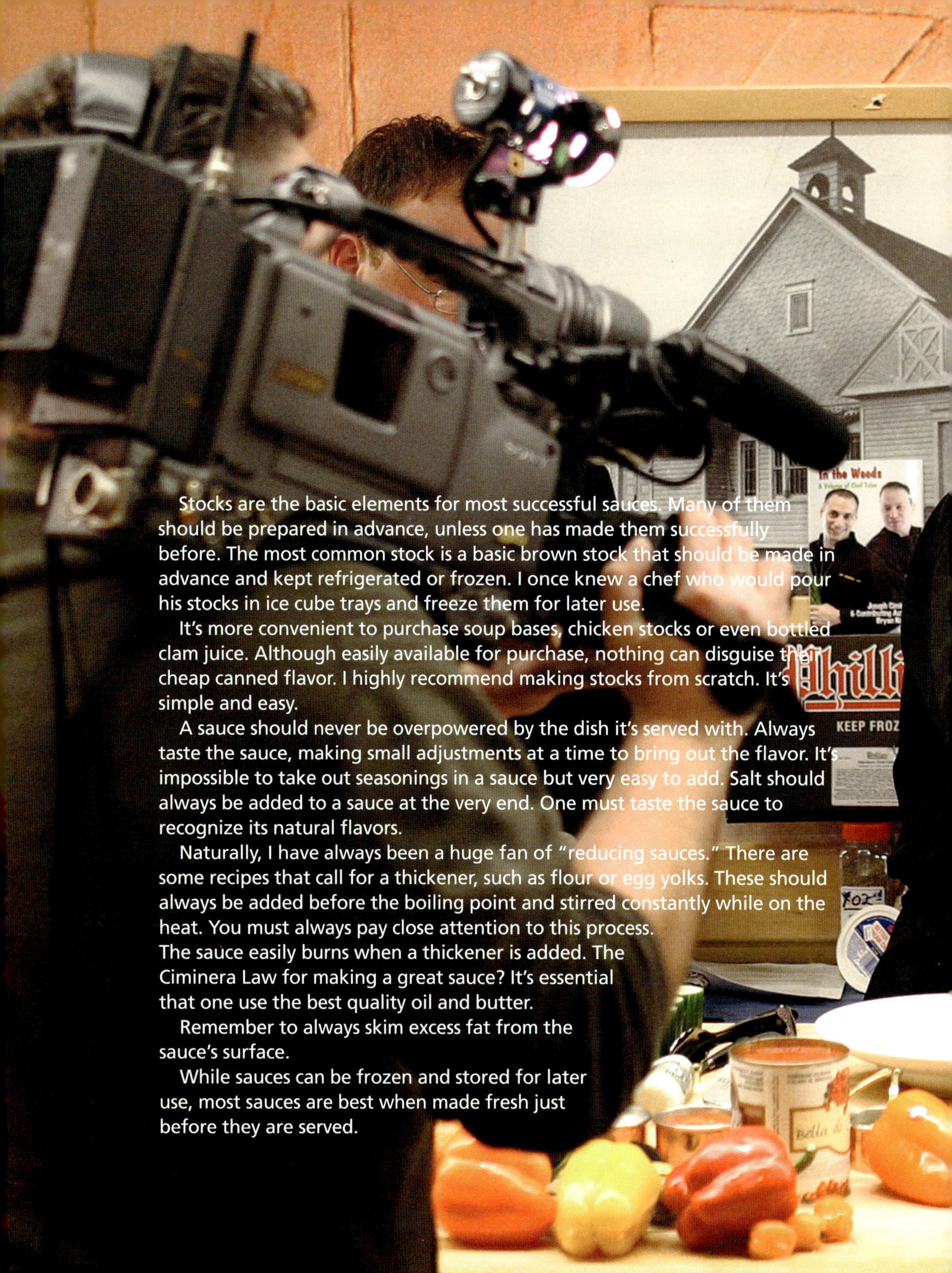

Stocks are the basic elements for most successful sauces. Many of them should be prepared in advance, unless one has made them successfully before. The most common stock is a basic brown stock that should be made in advance and kept refrigerated or frozen. I once knew a chef who would pour his stocks in ice cube trays and freeze them for later use.

It's more convenient to purchase soup bases, chicken stocks or even bottled clam juice. Although easily available for purchase, nothing can disguise their cheap canned flavor. I highly recommend making stocks from scratch. It's simple and easy.

A sauce should never be overpowered by the dish it's served with. Always taste the sauce, making small adjustments at a time to bring out the flavor. It's impossible to take out seasonings in a sauce but very easy to add. Salt should always be added to a sauce at the very end. One must taste the sauce to recognize its natural flavors.

Naturally, I have always been a huge fan of "reducing sauces." There are some recipes that call for a thickener, such as flour or egg yolks. These should always be added before the boiling point and stirred constantly while on the heat. You must always pay close attention to this process. The sauce easily burns when a thickener is added. The Ciminera Law for making a great sauce? It's essential that one use the best quality oil and butter.

Remember to always skim excess fat from the sauce's surface.

While sauces can be frozen and stored for later use, most sauces are best when made fresh just before they are served.

Sauces

Chicken Stock

5 quarts cold water
1 large roaster chicken, about 4 pounds and cut into 8 pieces
2 teaspoons salt
½ teaspoon whole peppercorns

For the bouquet garni
(the following herbs wrapped in cheesecloth and then tied):
1 fresh thyme sprig
1 parsley sprig
1 scallion
1 bay leaf
1 pound carrots, chopped
1 pound celery, chopped
1 leek, chopped
1 pound giblets (optional)
2 tablespoons Filippo Berio olive oil
1 cup dry white wine

For the chicken: Skin-side up in a roasting pan, brown the chicken and the giblets. Turn occasionally to ensure even browning. Roast at 450 degrees for 20 minutes. Deglaze the roasting pan with white wine. Reserve that liquid.

For the mire poix: In a large, heavy stockpot, add the 5 quarts of cold water. Add the browned chicken, the giblets and all the vegetables. Add the liquid from the roasting pan. Bring to a gentle simmer for 4 hours, skimming off the top of the stock occasionally. Do not stir the stock. After all the scum has been removed — and there is no sign of any more building up — remove the stock from the heat. Strain it through a cheesecloth. Discard the meat or save for later use in cold salads or hot soups. Taste and adjust the seasoning.

Yields three-fourths of a gallon.

Basic Brown Stock

1½ gallons water
4 thyme sprigs · 5 parsley sprigs
2 garlic cloves · 2 bay leaves
1 celery stalk, with leaves and roughly chopped
3 large white onions, roughly chopped
1 large red onion, roughly chopped
3 pounds large carrots, chopped
½-pound pork rind · 1 pound smoked ham
1 tablespoon butter
2 tablespoons Filippo Berio olive oil
1 pound beef shank
2 pounds veal shinbone
2 cups sweet red wine
8 ounces tomato paste
¼ teaspoon whole peppercorns
salt to taste

For the bones: Preheat the oven to 450 degrees. Place the bones in a large roasting pan. Turn and rotate the bones to ensure even cooking. The bones must be well browned, but do not burn them, as that will turn the stock bitter.

For the mire poix: In a heavy stockpot, melt the butter and olive oil over medium heat. Add the pork rind, ham, celery, carrots and onions. Continue to cook until the vegetables release their sugars and start to caramelize. Deglaze with the wine. Add 3 cups of water and tomato paste. Continue to reduce on low simmer. Add the bay leaves, salt, garlic, water, peppercorns, thyme and parsley. When the bones are brown, take them from the roasting pan. Add them to the stockpot. Strain the fat from the pan for a later use. Scrape all the browned bits from the pan. Add it into the stock. Continue to cook on low heat for 5 to 6 hours, always skimming the top to remove any scum that might form. Do not stir the stock, as it makes the stock cloudy. Adjust the flavoring if salt is needed. Remove the stock from the heat. While it's still hot, strain it through a cheesecloth or China cap more than once.

For demi-glaze: Reduce the stock further by boiling until it gets a syrupy consistency. Be careful not to burn the stock as it thickens. Demi-glaze can be frozen and used later. It's great for soup or flavoring sauces.

Yields three-fourths of a gallon.

Blond Roux

Melt 3 tablespoons of butter in a pan over medium heat. Stir in 3 tablespoons of flour. Simmer for 3 or 4 minutes, but do not allow the mixture to brown. A cup of stock or liquid should be added to this mixture. Constantly stir on the burner until the sauce has thickened.

Chef's note: The method is to add cold liquid very gradually to the cooking butter and flour.

Bing Cherry Reduction

2 pounds Bing cherries, stemmed and pitted
2 cups hot water
1 tablespoon lemon zest
1 tablespoon orange zest
½ tablespoon agar-agar
1 ounce Grand Marnier liqueur
2 large carrots, peeled
1½ sticks cinnamon
¼ cup orange juice
1 tablespoon granulated sugar
cheesecloth to strain sauce

For the cherries: Wash them thoroughly in cold water to remove any dirt. On medium heat, place a 2-quart heavy saucepan. Add the cherries and cinnamon sticks. Pour hot water over the cherries to cover them. Add the orange zest, sugar and lemon zest to the pan. When the cherries have absorbed most of the water, remove them from the burner. In a blender, puree the cherries on high speed until well blended. Place the puree back into the saucepan. Add the Grand Marnier and orange juice. Bring the puree back to a simmer. Continue to cook for 12 minutes on medium heat. Remove the puree from the heat. Strain it through the cheesecloth. Squeeze the cloth tightly to get all the juice. Return the strained sauce to the pan. Bring the sauce to a simmer again. Add the agar-agar. Blend with a whisk. When the sauce thickens, take it off the heat.

Chef's note: Agar-agar is made from seaweed and is used for thickening sauces. If you are unable to find it, substitute arrowroot powder. To improve the sauce's body, melt a tablespoon of unsalted butter into the hot sauce.

Carrot Sauce

2 pounds peeled carrots, diced
2 cups rice wine vinegar
1 pint orange juice · 2 pints water
1 pint white wine
salt and white pepper to taste

For the sauce: In large, heavy pot, put all the ingredients together. Simmer them until the carrots are completely soft. In a large blender or food processor, blend the carrots and liquid together until very smooth (roughly 10 minutes).

Uses for the sauce: This sauce is good for grilled or poached fish and can also be used as a sauce for vegetables.

Porcini Mushroom Sauce

2 cups fresh porcini (you can substitute with dry or frozen)
½ cup Filippo Berio olive oil
8 fresh basil leaves
3 fresh garlic cloves, minced
1 cup dry white wine
1 fresh sage sprig, minced
2 tablespoons green peppercorns, in the brine
1½ cup heavy cream
1 cup demi-glaze (see demi-glaze recipe)
1 shallot bulb, diced
½ cup brandy

For the sauce: In a large double-enamel pot on medium, heat the oil. Add the shallots, garlic and porcini mushrooms. Sauté until the onions are brown. Add the fresh sage and basil. Continue to cook for another minute to release the herbs' flavor. Take the pot off the heat. Add the brandy (caution: it will flame!). Place the pot back on the burner. Add the white wine. When the liquid has reduced by half, add the peppercorns, the demi-glaze and the heavy cream. Continue to cook the mixture down by three-fourths. The result should be a reduced sauce thick enough to coat a spoon's back.

Chef's note: This versatile sauce can be used in almost all beef and veal dishes. I have found that the sauce is just as good if not better on some freshly cooked pasta. Try that one with a little shaved Parmigiano-Reggiano cheese on top. I perfected this dish in Italy some years ago when I was working in a hotel outside Milan. Since then, the sauce has been a real crowd-pleaser.

Whole Cranberry Orange Sauce

1 12-ounce package fresh cranberries
1 cup sugar
1½ cups orange juice
2 tablespoons orange marmalade
¼ cup pecans, chopped
¼ teaspoon cinnamon
¼ teaspoon white pepper

For the sauce: Wash cranberries. Dry them well. In a medium saucepan, mix the orange juice, sugar and berries. Place the mixture on medium heat. Bring it to a boil. Stir frequently. When the berries begin to pop, add the remaining ingredients. Mix well. When the sauce starts to thicken, remove it from the heat. Pour it into a bowl to refrigerate.

For the plate: Cranberry sauce is the perfect accompaniment for roast meats. Serve it on holidays with turkey, roast beef, duck or any other festive dish.

When making bread, be sure to use bread flour. It contains more gluten than other flours, such as all-purpose. Used to make breads of any kind, bread flour usually requires more yeast and is slower in rising. This flour should always be sifted at least once before measuring and once before mixing.

Yeast can either be fresh or dried and stored in dated envelopes. Fresh yeast should be dissolved in warm water that is no higher than 80 degrees. Liquid for dissolving dry yeast should be about 100 to 110 degrees. Wait for the yeast to foam after mixing it with warm water.

The temperature that leavened dough is set to rise at is extremely important. It should be away from sudden drafts and not be next to either a hot or cold atmosphere. Before putting the dough in a bowl to rise, be sure to lightly rub shortening throughout the bowl and to the top of the dough. This will prevent a crust from forming, and it permits the necessary gluten development. Cover the bowl lightly with a towel or plastic wrap. Leavened dough will rise best at 85 degrees. Set the dough to rise in a warm place — away from any sudden climate changes.

Excessive kneading might result in a tougher product. As dough is kneaded, it becomes more elastic and less sticky. If more flour is needed, add a little underneath and on top of the dough.

Appetizers and Breads

Smashed Potatoes with Four Onions

3 pounds Yukon Gold potatoes, skin on and cut into quarters
¼ cup canola oil
1 large red onion, cut into large dice
1 garlic head, unpeeled
4 tablespoons unsalted butter
2 leeks, white part only and cut into small strips
1 bunch chives
¼ pound unsalted butter, cut into small pieces and very cold
2 cups heavy cream
kosher salt for water
salt and white pepper to taste

For the onions: Heat canola oil in a sauté pan, and when hot, place the red onions in it. Lower the heat. Sauté the onions until they turn brown. Remove them from pan to cool. Melt 1 tablespoon of butter in the same sauté pan. Add leeks, cooking until well browned. Preheat the oven to 400 degrees. Trim off the garlic head. Place it in a shallow baking dish with some water in the bottom. Top the garlic with butter. Roast in an oven until the garlic is very soft. Remove it from oven. When cool, break the cloves off the head. Squeeze out and reserve the roasted garlic. Discard the skins. Cut the chives very finely. Put them aside.

For the potatoes: Put the potatoes in a large pot. Cover them completely with cold water. Season generously with kosher salt. Place the pot on the stove. Bring the water to a boil. Cook the potatoes until they're are soft but not falling apart. Drain the water. While the potatoes are still hot, place them in a mixing bowl to break them up. Slowly add the remaining cold butter and cream. Add salt and white pepper to taste. When the potatoes become fluffy, stop mixing. Fold in the red onion, roasted garlic and leeks by hand. When blended well and creamy, place the mixture in a serving dish.

For the plate: Sprinkle the chopped chives on top. Serve immediately.

Serves 8.

Basil Pesto

1 cup fresh basil leaves
8 flat-leaf or Italian parsley sprigs
1 bunch fresh sage
1 cup Parmigiano-Reggiano cheese, grated
¼ cup pine nuts
1 cup cashew nuts
1 cup spinach, washed and diced
4 garlic cloves, roasted
4 tablespoons Filippo Berio olive oil
2 tablespoons truffle oil
sea salt to taste

Chef's note: The best way to make this recipe is to use a mortar or just pulse the ingredients in a food processor. This recipe has a shelf life of 5 days.

Sun-Dried Tomato Pesto

2 cups sun-dried tomatoes
4 garlic cloves, roasted
¼ cup pine nuts
¼ cup cashew nuts
2 tablespoons tomato paste
1 cup Parmigiano-Reggiano cheese, grated
sea salt to taste

Chef's note: In a food processor, blend all the ingredients until they reach a thick paste consistency. Be careful not to overblend the pesto. It has a tendency to heat up and set the cheese off in an unpleasant reaction. This recipe has a shelf life of 1 week.

Braised Red Cabbage with Apples

1 red cabbage head
3 Granny Smith apples, skinned and diced
4 tablespoons unsalted butter
1 cup light brown sugar
2 cups apple cider vinegar
salt and pepper to taste

For the cabbage: Split the cabbage in half, removing the center core with a paring knife. Wash the cabbage in cold running water. Shred the cabbage thinly with a knife or use a grater. Core the apples. Cut them into wedges, leaving the skin on.

To braise the cabbage and apples: Melt butter in a large cast-iron pan or skillet. Add the cabbage. Toss the cabbage to mix the butter through. Add salt and pepper. Cook on moderate heat for 10 minutes, stirring often to avoid browning the cabbage. Add the brown sugar. Stir it through to melt. Add the vinegar. Reduce the heat to low, continuing to stir often. If liquid gets low, add more vinegar or water. After 15 minutes, add the apples to the pan. Cook for another 15 to 20 minutes or until the cabbage is very limp and the apples are soft.

For the plate: This is an excellent side dish for roasted meats and game. It also goes well on a sandwich. Its sweet and sour taste can be enjoyed either hot or cold.

Sweet Pea Wasabi

1 bag frozen sweet peas
1 cup breadcrumbs
1 tablespoon sea salt
1 tablespoon white pepper
4 garlic cloves, roasted
3 marjoram sprigs
1 teaspoon hot sauce

Chef's note: In a food processor, mix all the ingredients until all the flavors are evenly distributed. Chill immediately. This recipe only has a shelf life of 1 day, so make what you need.

Best Damn Coleslaw

1 large green cabbage head
3 cups apple cider vinegar
½ cup mayonnaise
½ cup sour cream
½ cup canola oil
1 tablespoon white pepper
2 tablespoons kosher salt
1 teaspoon crab seasoning
hot sauce

For the slaw: Wash the cabbage. Cut it in half, removing the core. Cut it into quarters. Shred the cabbage with a knife or grater into thin shreds. Place in a large bowl.

For the dressing: Combine the apple cider vinegar, mayonnaise, sour cream and all the seasonings in a mixing bowl. Slowly whisk in the canola oil until the mixture is slightly thickened. Pour the dressing over the cabbage. Mix it in thoroughly. Press a dish on top of the slaw. Place a weight over the dish. Refrigerate for at least 3 hours, but overnight is best.

Chef's note: This is how coleslaw should be done — no carrots or anything else to cripple the cabbage's crispness and the dressing's tang. Stir well before serving. This is great with barbeque meats as a sandwich.

Green Beans and Red Onions

5 medium-sized red onions
¼ cup Filippo Berio olive oil
2 tablespoons good-quality balsamic vinegar
1 teaspoon kosher salt
½ teaspoon black pepper
¼ cup vegetable stock
1½-pounds green beans, trimmed and cut on bias into 2-inch pieces

For the onions: Peel and trim the onions. Cut into quarters lengthwise. Place the onions in a bowl. Pour olive oil and balsamic vinegar on them. Season with salt and pepper. Place them on a baking sheet cut-side down. Cook them in a preheated 450 degree oven for 15 minutes. Turn the onions. Add the vegetable stock. Cook for another 15 minutes or until the onions start to caramelize.

For the green beans: Place the beans in rapidly boiling, salted water. Cook until al dente. Drain the green beans from the water. Pour them onto the baking sheet with the onions. Mix thoroughly, place back in the oven and then cook for another 10 minutes. Remove them from oven. Serve immediately.

Serves 6 to 8.

Dual-Potato Polenta

2 Yukon Gold potatoes · 2 sweet potatoes
¼ cup bresaola (an Italian air-cured beef), diced
¼ teaspoon white pepper · ¼ cup lard · 2 shallots
2 tablespoons "00" flour or pastry flour · 4 ounces prosciutto di Parma, diced
1 cup fresh tarragon, chopped · salt and white pepper to taste

For the polenta: Peel the potatoes before cutting them into small pieces. Bring them to a boil in salted water. When the potatoes are soft, press them through a potato ricer. Set aside. In a heavy-bottom pot, melt the lard to sauté the prosciutto, bresaola and shallots. Stir in the flour. Mix until smooth and lump-free. Add the riced potatoes and tarragon. Season with salt and white pepper, stirring well.

For the plate: The polenta can be finished two ways. Spread it evenly in a baking dish. Bake in a 350 oven until browned on top. Or press it into ring molds on a baking sheet. Brown in the oven as previously described, but before removing it from the oven, cover the tops with shredded Parmigiano-Reggiano cheese.

Potato Cake

2 pounds Idaho potatoes, cleaned and peeled · 1 fresh thyme sprig, leaves only
2 tablespoons Filippo Berio olive oil · 2 tablespoons butter
1 shallot, diced · 10 brown organic eggs
¼ cup fresh chives, minced · 6 ounces fresh mozzarella, shredded
½ cup Parmigiano-Reggiano cheese, grated · 1 teaspoon flour
½ cup Asiago cheese, grated · salt and pepper to taste

For the potatoes: Place the potatoes in a 6-quart pot. Fill the pot with cold water until the potatoes are covered. Heat on high until the water reaches a boil. After 10 minutes, lower the heat down to medium. Poke each potato's center with a toothpick. When they are tender, drain the potatoes. Put them in the refrigerator for 13 minutes.

For the custard: In a bowl, break the eggs into a bowl. Whip the eggs until well blended. Add the shallots, thyme and the three cheeses. Continue to mix. Add the chives and flour, constantly mixing until all the custard is incorporated.

For the cake: Have the potatoes ready by slicing them into thin rounds in a half-dollar shape. In a skillet on medium heat, add the oil and melt the butter until slightly brown. Layer the sliced potatoes in the pan about one-quarter up the pan's sides. Reduce the heat to low. Top the potatoes with one-quarter of the custard. Place another layer of potatoes in the pan to reach the halfway level. Add more custard mixture. Repeat the process until the potatoes reach three-quarters full in the pan. Sprinkle the top with grated Parmigiano-Reggiano cheese. Place the cake in a 350 degree oven for 30 minutes until golden brown on top.

Pizza at Its Best

3¾ cups sifted bread flour
1 ounce wet yeast · 1 teaspoon salt
1 tablespoon honey
1 cup warm water, at 100 to 110 degrees
¼ cup Filippo Berio olive oil
1½-pound whole cherry tomatoes, peeled, seeded, drained and julienned
3 garlic cloves, roasted
2 tablespoons fresh oregano or 2 teaspoons dried oregano
3 ounces prosciutto, sliced and chopped
1 pound fresh imported buffalo milk mozzarella, diced
¼ cup Parmigiano-Reggiano cheese, grated
1 bottle 25-year-old balsamic vinegar
salt and freshly ground pepper

For the dough: Sift the flour onto a wooden board. Mold a mountain of flour with a little hole in the center. Dissolve the yeast in warm water. Be sure it's warm, not hot. Hot water will kill the yeast. Add the salt and honey. Let the yeast multiply for 13 minutes. Pour a little bit of warm water into the flour's center, gently working the flour with your fingers. Eventually, work all the water and flour together, roll the dough into a ball and then cover it in a bowl. Let it rest in a warm area until it doubles in size. Lightly flour a board. Knead the dough until it holds shape. Divide the dough into four equal parts. Roll each section into a complete circle about ⅛-inch thick and 8 inches in diameter. Be sure that the edges are a bit bigger to form the crust. Brush the dough with some oil. Let it sit for 4 minutes.

For the sauce: In a bowl, put the tomatoes in first. Mix in the oregano, garlic and grated Parmigiano-Reggiano cheese.

For the assembly: Generously grease a pan. Spread the dough into the pan. With a ladle, evenly distribute the sauce over the pizza dough. Add the buffalo mozzarella and prosciutto. Season with salt and pepper. Bake in the oven at 425 degrees for 15 minutes. Drizzle aged balsamic vinegar on top!

Serves 7.

Recommended wines:
Lindemans Shiraz Reserve (Hunter Valley, Australia)
Hogue Syrah 2002 (Washington State, USA)

Peasant Bread

The sponge:
½ envelope active dry yeast
2½ tablespoons warm water, at 113 degrees
⅓ cup plus 2 tablespoons warm water
1⅛ cup bread flour

The dough:
½ teaspoon wet yeast
3 tablespoons warm milk, at 113 degrees
¾ cup warm water · 2 tablespoon olive oil
2 cups bread flour · 1½ teaspoons salt · ½ cup "00" flour

Special equipment: You will need a baking stone for this recipe.

For the sponge: In a stainless steel bowl, stir together the yeast and 2½ tablespoons of warm water. Let the mixture stand for 4 minutes or until creamy. In a bowl, stir together the yeast mixture and the room-temperature water and flour. Stir for 5 minutes. Cover the bowl with plastic wrap, making sure that the plastic is sealed well. Let the sponge stand at a cool room temperature for 1 day.

For the dough: In a small bowl, stir together the yeast and milk. Let the mixture stand for 4 minutes or until it's foamy. In the bowl of a stand mixer fitted with a dough hook, blend the sponge together with the milk mixture, water, oil and flour at low speed until the flour is just moistened. Beat the dough at medium speed for 2 minutes. Add salt. Beat for 5 more minutes. Scrape the dough into an oiled bowl covered with plastic wrap. Let the dough rise at room temperature for about 2 hours until it has doubled in bulk.

To bake the bread: Prepare a baking sheet and two well-floured 12-inch by 6-inch sheets of parchment paper. Put the dough on a well-floured work surface, cutting the dough in half. Transfer each half to a parchment sheet. Form the dough into an irregular oval about 10 inches long. Cover the loaves with a dampened kitchen towel. Let the loaves rise at room temperature for approximately 2 hours until it has almost doubled in bulk. At least 40 minutes before baking the peasant bread, put a baking stone on an oven rack in the lowest position within the oven, preheating it to 425 degrees. Transfer 1 loaf on its parchment to a rimless baking sheet, with the loaf's long side parallel to the baking sheet's far edge. Line up the baking sheet's far edge with a stone or tiles. Tilt the baking sheet to slide the loaf with parchment onto the back half of a stone or tiles. Transfer the remaining loaf to the front half of a stone or tiles in a similar manner. Bake the loaves for 20 minutes or until pale gold.

Yields 2 to 3 loaves.

Basic Bread Dough

4 cups all-purpose flour
1 ounce plus ¼ teaspoon wet yeast
⅔ cup olive oil
½ cup whole milk
2 teaspoons salt

For the dough: Warm the milk to 100 degrees to dissolve the yeast. Set aside for 11 minutes. Sift the flour into a bowl. Make a small well in the center — the same procedure that is used to make pasta. Add the oil and the salt to the milk. Slowly pour the milk into the center, working the dough very slowly. When the flour and the milk are incorporated, knead for about 20 minutes, dusting the board often to avoid sticking. Place the soft dough into a covered bowl. Put the bowl in a warm area for 2½ hours. When the dough has raised, pat it down. Roll it into the desired shape.

Chef's note: This dough can be used for a variety of purposes, including pizza.

Buttermilk Blue Cheese Bread

3 pounds flour
2 envelopes dry yeast
3½ cups warm water
1 fresh oregano sprig, minced
2 tablespoons Filippo Berio olive oil
2 whole and 1 yolk brown organic eggs
1 pound Roth Käse Buttermilk Blue Cheese, crumbled
¼ cup plus 1 teaspoon salt
1 tablespoon cracked black pepper

Special equipment: Two half-sheet pans

For the starter: In a bowl, combine three-fourths of a cup of warm water and the yeast, dissolving the yeast until it's well incorporated. Add 1 pound of flour. Mix until all the flour has been absorbed by the water. Cover the bowl with plastic wrap. Let the mixture rise. It should at least double in size.

For the dough: Lay the remaining flour on a wooden cutting board or a flat surface. Make a hole in the center — the same way you would start to make pasta. In the center, slowly mix in the water, oil and salt. Make sure you knead the dough well. If it's too sticky, add a little bit more flour.

For the cheese: In a bowl, whisk the eggs. Add the crumbled buttermilk cheese, minced oregano and cracked black pepper. Pour the contents into the bowl with the starter. Add the dough on top of the cheese mixture. Knead the components together until fully incorporated. Again, if it's too sticky, add a bit more flour.

For the baking: Thoroughly oil the half-sheet pans. Split the dough in half. Place one-half of the dough in each pan's center. Let it proof again for about 1½ hours. Make sure to cover the dough with plastic wrap. Keep in a warm area. When the dough has proofed, carefully push the dough down with your fingertips so that it's even in the pan. Add a considerable amount of oil on the top of the dough, rubbing it all over with your hands. Preheat the oven to 410 degrees. Bake for about 25 minutes.

Yields 2 loaves.

Buttermilk Cheddar Biscuits

1¾ cups all-purpose flour
¾ cup fine cornmeal
4 teaspoons baking powder
1 teaspoon baking soda
1 teaspoon salt
½ stick unsalted butter, very cold and cut into half-inch pieces
6 ounces cheddar cheese, grated
1⅓ cups buttermilk

For the batter: Sift all the dry ingredients together in a mixing bowl. With your hands or a pastry blender, blend in the butter until the mix resembles wet sand. Stir in the cheddar cheese with a wooden spoon. Add the buttermilk. Stir until just combined.

To bake the biscuits: With a tablespoon, drop the dough onto a baking sheet. Use all the dough. Bake in a preheated 450 degree oven for 15 minutes or until golden. Remove the biscuits from the pan. Allow them to cool slightly. Serve them while they're still very warm.

Yields 8 to 10 biscuits.

Pasta an

BOLLA
PINOT GRIGIO
Taste
Risotto

Basic Pasta Dough

2 cups all-purpose flour
½ cup "00" flour
3 whole brown eggs · 1 egg yolk
1 teaspoon Filippo Berio olive oil
1 tablespoon whole milk
¼ teaspoon salt

For the pasta: Sift the flour on a pastry board or a flat working surface. Shape the flour into a mound, with a well in the center. Start by breaking 1 whole egg into the well. Using a fork, break the egg into the flour, incorporating it gradually. After working the first egg in, knead the other eggs into the flour. Add the remaining ingredients. Work the dough until smooth and elastic, cut the dough in half to let out any air in the dough and then wrap it for 17 minutes. Lightly flour a board. Flatten the dough out with a rolling pin, working outward from the center and rotating it each time to form a circle. Let the dough sit another 5 minutes. Pass it through a pasta machine for the desired shape. If you use the dough for any kind of stuffed pasta, cut it into shape and stuff immediately to avoid the pasta from becoming too dry.

My Version of Macaroni and Cheese

Dough:
4 cups all-purpose flour
6 brown organic eggs
2 tablespoons Filippo Berio olive oil
1 tablespoon milk
3 tablespoons Parmigiano-Reggiano cheese, grated
¼ teaspoon black pepper

Sauce:
1 can whole summer black truffles
3 ounces Boschetto al Tartufo truffle cheese
2 tablespoons Filippo Berio olive oil
1 tablespoon truffle oil
½ cup Parmigiano-Reggiano cheese, grated
1 tablespoon chives, minced · 4 ounces butter, unsalted
1 tablespoon sheep's milk ricotta
salt and freshly cracked black pepper to taste

For the dough: Make a flour mound on a pastry board, with a hole in the mound's center. Crack the eggs one at a time into the dough's center. Add the cheese, black pepper, oil and milk. Bring the dough together to form a ball. Let it rest for 2 hours, covered in a cool spot in the kitchen. Flour a board to roll the dough flat — about one-fourth of an inch thick. Cut desired shapes from the pasta. Cook the noodles in vigorously boiling, salted water until they are al dente. Strain the pasta. Toss it with oil to prevent sticking.

For the sauce: In a medium saucepan, heat the butter and the olive oil to cook the truffles for 2 minutes. Add the pasta. Remove the saucepan from the heat. Toss the Boschetto al Tartufo cheese, the Parmigiano-Reggiano and the chives in with the pasta. Season with salt and pepper. Stir in the truffle oil. Just before serving, garnish each plate with a spoon of sheep's milk ricotta.

Chef's note: Sheep's milk ricotta, canned black truffles and truffle cheese are all available from The Chef's Warehouse in the Bronx, New York. If you can't get sheep's milk ricotta, use cow's milk ricotta, which is available in almost every supermarket. Remember: There are no rules in cooking.

Recommended wines:

Fontana Candida Pinot Grigio (Lazio, Italy)
Korbel Brut (Sonoma County, California, USA)

Green Risotto with Bacon and Parmesan Cheese

2 cups Arborio rice
1 cup Parmigiano-Reggiano cheese, grated
6 cups chicken stock
4 ounces parsley leaves
1 ounce fresh basil
1 shallot, minced
2 tablespoons butter
2 tablespoons Filippo Berio olive oil
2 ounces bacon, diced
1 cup dry white wine
salt and freshly ground pepper

For the parsley sauce: Heat 4 cups of chicken stock with the parsley and the basil for 10 minutes. Pour into a blender, puree for about 5 minutes and then set the mixture aside.

For the risotto: Melt 2 tablespoons of butter in a heavy-bottom pot over medium heat. Add the shallots and bacon. Cook until both are transparent. Deglaze with the wine, reducing all the way down until it has just about evaporated. Add the Arborio rice, turning it slowly with a wooden spoon. Make sure all the rice has been coated with the butter and wine reduction. Add 2 cups of chicken stock. Reduce slightly. Add salt and pepper to taste. Remember that the chicken stock will reduce, but the salinity will increase. Add the remainder of chicken stock and parsley. Continue to cook for about 18 minutes or until the rice has released its starch and is smooth and creamy. Take the pan off the heat to add the cheese. Mix thoroughly. Add the parsley sauce.

Chef's note: Risotto can be used as a separate course or as a side dish. Always have extra grated cheese on hand for your guests.

Recommended wines:
Sonoma Cutrer Russian River Ranches Chardonnay 2002 (Russian River, Sonoma, California, USA)
Michel Picard Sancerre 2003 (Loire, France)

White Truffle Risotto with Roth Käse Gran Cru Gruyère Cheese

12 ounces Carnaroli or Arborio rice
6 ounces unsalted butter
½ onion, finely chopped
1 quart-plus chicken stock
6 ounces Roth Käse Gran Cru Gruyère cheese, cut into small dice
2 tablespoons white truffle shavings, fresh preferred (canned if necessary)
kosher salt and white pepper to taste
2 tablespoons Italian parsley, chopped
white truffle oil to finish

For the risotto: Melt butter in a heavy-bottom saucepan. Do not burn. Sweat the onion in the butter. Do not brown the onion. Add the rice, coating it well with the butter and onion. Begin adding the chicken stock slowly. As the liquid absorbs, add more stock until the rice is cooked to al dente. Add the Gruyère, mixing it into the risotto until melted. Add the truffle shavings and parsley. Mix them, adjust the salt and pepper and then remove the saucepan from the heat.

For the plate: Risotto can be used as a separate course or as a side dish. Before serving, drizzle white truffle oil around the plate. Garnish with an Italian parsley sprig.

Serves 4.

Garganelli Pasta Ragout with Prosciutto and Eggplant

2 pounds DeCecco Garganelli pasta
2 tablespoons bacon, diced
2 tablespoons prosciutto, diced
2 tablespoons pancetta, diced
1 shallot, diced
3 tablespoons Filippo Berio olive oil
1 cup red sweet wine
1 pound tomatoes, peeled and seeded
1 bunch fresh basil
2 medium eggplants, peeled, thinly sliced and pressed under a weight for 2 hours
1½-pound Parmigiano-Reggiano cheese, grated
1 pound yellow tomatoes, peeled and seeded
2 tablespoons unsalted butter
salt and black pepper to taste

For the pasta: Bring a large pot of salted water to a boil. Slowly add the pasta. Cook for 9 minutes or until al dente. Drain. Add the pasta to the sauce.

For the sauce: In a heavy saucepan on high heat, add the oil, shallots, pancetta, prosciutto and bacon until well cooked and slightly brown. Add the fresh basil. Continue to cook until the leaves become wilted. Add the eggplants, stirring constantly until they have released some of their water and are soft. Add the wine. Cook until the wine is completely evaporated. Add the red and yellow tomatoes until the eggplants are covered. Continue cooking for 1½ hours on low simmer. Add the cheese and the butter. Remove the sauce from the heat. Mix it well with the pasta.

Serves 6 to 8.

Recommended wines:
Bolla Tufave (Soave, Italy)
Albarino Villareui 2001 (Rias Baixas, Spain)

Torchia Pasta

1 stick high-fat unsalted butter
1 cup prosciutto di Parma, cut into small dice
1 tablespoon Filippo Berio olive oil
½ cup fresh vine ripened tomatoes, seeded and diced
½ cup fresh basil, whole
6 shallots, thinly sliced
3 garlic cloves, sliced
1⅓ cups light cream or half-and-half
1 quart heavy cream
4 1½-pound lobsters, steamed and meat removed from shells
12 ounces DeCecco Orecchiette
¼ cup Parmigiano-Reggiano cheese (about 1 ounce), freshly grated
1 cup white wine (Pinot Grigio is preferred)

For the lobster sauce: Melt butter in a heavy, large skillet over medium-high heat. Add the olive oil, prosciutto, shallots and garlic. Cook until golden brown and the prosciutto's color has been rendered into the oil. Deglaze with wine. Reduce by half. Add heavy cream. Reduce by half again. When the cream is thick and bubbling, add the lobster meat and tomatoes. Finally, before serving the dish, add the grated Parmigiano-Reggiano cheese. Stir the sauce evenly off the heat. The heat will pull the cheese to the pan's bottom and burn it if you're not careful. Keep warm until ready to serve.

For the pasta: Meanwhile, cook the pasta in a large pot of boiling, salted water until al dente. The pasta will cook in 10 to 12 minutes, depending on the pasta's size.

For the dish: On low heat, add the cooked pasta to the pan. Continue to mix for 1 minute. Take the pan off the heat before adding the whipping cream. Enjoy!

Recommended wines:
Bolla Pinot Grigio (Trentino, Italy)
Mezzacorana Reserve Pinot Grigio (Trentino, Italy)

Taste This!
FONTINA

Carnaroli Risotto with Braised Pork and White Truffles

Pork:
1 pound pork shoulder, boned, fat removed, rolled and tied
2 quarts red wine
4 tablespoons tomato paste
1 shallot, peeled and diced
1 bay leaf · salt and pepper to taste
½ cup Filippo Berio olive oil

Risotto:
2 teaspoons butter · 1½ teaspoons lard
½ shallot bulb, peeled and diced
1 cup white wine
2 cups Carnaroli risotto · 5 cups chicken stock
2 ounces Pecorino Romano cheese, grated
1 ounce white truffle oil · salt and pepper to taste

For the pork: In a skillet on medium heat, add the olive oil. Cook the oil until it's smoking hot. Place the pork roll in the pan, browning evenly on all sides. Take the pork from the skillet, but discard the oil. Return the pot back to the stove — along with the pork — and deglaze with red wine. Add the shallot, bay leaf and the tomato paste. Braise on simmer for about 1 hour and 45 minutes, checking the meat's tenderness every 15 minutes. When the pork is done, take the string off. Keep warm until ready to serve.

For the risotto: Melt the butter and the lard in a large pot. Add the diced shallot. Cook until translucent. Add the wine. Bring the mixture to a boil. Lower the heat to stir in the rice, constantly turning the rice to avoid sticking to the pan's bottom. Add the stock 1 cup at a time, adding more when the rice has absorbed the liquid. When the rice has released its starch and is al dente, remove it from the heat. Add the cheese, truffle oil and the salt to taste.

For the plate: Cut the pork into thick slices. Place the risotto on a large platter, arranging the pork around it. Garnish with fresh parsley and basil.

Chef's note: Don't be afraid to use lard. It actually has less saturated fat than butter and adds a tremendous amount of flavor.

Recommended wines:
Robert Mondavi Napa Pinot Noir 2001 (Napa Valley, California, USA)
Bolla Le Poiane Valpolicella Classico (Veneto, Italy)

Pumpkin Risotto

1½ cups pumpkin puree or butternut squash puree
2½ cups Arborio rice
½ cup onion, chopped
3 tablespoons Filippo Berio olive oil
3 tablespoons unsalted butter
2 quarts white chicken stock
½ cup heavy cream
½ cup Parmigiano-Reggiano
salt and pepper to taste

For the risotto: Melt butter in a heavy pot on medium heat. Stir the olive oil into the butter. Add the onions to the pot. Sauté them until they're limp but not brown. Add the rice to the pot, stirring with a wooden spoon to coat the rice well. Do not brown the rice. Start to add the chicken stock slowly. Stir the rice until the liquid has been absorbed. Add more stock. Keep repeating this process. As the rice cooks, it will release its starch and become creamy. When the rice is partly cooked, add the pumpkin puree. Stir well. Season with salt and pepper. The rice should be al dente when cooked. Add the cream and Parmigiano-Reggiano. Mix them into the rice.

For the plate: The risotto can be served as a side dish for meats or as a separate course. Garnish with shreds of Parmigiano-Reggiano and sage leaves.

Fedelini Pasta with Geoduck Clams

1 pound cockle clams
2 geoduck clams, frozen
(this is a very large clam that needs to be specially ordered)
12 fresh basil leaves
1 bunch chives, diced
2 plum tomatoes, seeded and diced
6 garlic cloves
1 cup white wine
1 pound fedelini pasta
1 tablespoon high-fat butter
salt and pepper to taste

For the pasta: In a pasta pot with half water and half white wine that has been salted, add the pasta. Cook it until it's until al dente (or for about 10 minutes). Strain. Set aside. Be sure to add just a bit of olive oil over the pasta to ensure it does not stick. It will also add a good flavor to the dish. Spread the hot pasta over an oiled sheet tray so that it cools evenly.

For the clam preparation: Take the frozen clams from the shell. Lay them on a cutting board. Remove the muscle on the clam. It looks round and tan, like a cylinder. The clam will defrost very quickly. When it does, slice it thinly. Retain all the juices. Rinse the cockle clams thoroughly at least six times to ensure all the sand is off.

For the sauce: In a saucepan, heat the oil on high until it's hot. Add the whole garlic. Cook it until it's brown. Add the cockle clams and the fresh basil. Deglaze with the white wine. Reduce by half. Add the sliced clams and the diced tomatoes. Cook for 5 minutes. Check the sauce for salt and pepper. Add the pasta to the sauce, along with the fresh chives and butter.

Advice: If you have ever tried to shuck open a geoduck, it's difficult. I recommend freezing the clam for 8 hours and then defrosting them. By freezing the clam, it weakens its muscles, therefore releasing the clam to open by itself. If you cannot find the prized geoduck, buy large cherrystones. Fedelini is spaghetti-shaped pasta from Italy. If you can't find it, substitute linguine or angel hair.

Recommended wines:
Batasiolo Gavi di Gavi 2002 White (Piedmont, Italy)
Gigi Rosso Roero Arneis 2002 White (Piedmont, Italy)

Mascarpone Gnocchi

5 pints whole milk
4 ounces butter, melted
1 tablespoon salt
4 tablespoons Filippo Berio olive oil
4 egg yolks, beaten
16 ounces all-purpose flour, sifted
1½ cups mascarpone cheese

For the gnocchi: In a stand mixer with the dough hook attachment, combine the salt and flour on a slow speed. In a separate bowl, combine the butter, milk and olive oil. To prevent lumps, add the milk mixture in a slow, steady stream to the mixer. Add the cheese and egg yolks. Let the mixer run until the mixture is smooth. On a floured table, put the dough from the bowl. Roll the dough into half-inch-thick logs about 6 inches long. Cut on a bias about an inch long. You should end up with individual pieces 1-inch by half-inch. Refrigerate until firm (about 1 hour). In salted, rapidly boiling water, add the gnocchi a few at a time. When they float to the top, the gnocchi are done. Remove them from the pot. Serve immediately with your favorite sauce or chill in an ice bath for later use.

About gnocchi: Gnocchi are very versatile. They can become a great lunch — sautéed in a little extra virgin olive oil with a sprinkle of Parmigiano-Reggiano — or the perfect accompaniment to a seductive braised meat or stew. Gnocchi can be made in a variety of ways by substituting other soft cheeses, such as Boursin or ricotta. Try adding some fresh herbs, such as basil or oregano. In my restaurant, I once added mint and served it with braised lamb shanks. It was a winner. Remember: There are no rules in cooking.

Strozzapreti Ragout with Black Truffles

1 ounce black truffle peelings · 1 ounce white truffle oil
1 ounce mascarpone cheese
8 fresh basil leaves
2 ounces Parmigiano-Reggiano cheese, grated
2 cups red wine (to add to the pasta's cooking water) plus 2 cups for the sauce
2 ounces ground pork · 2 ounces ground beef · 2 ounces ground veal
½ cup heavy cream
2 tablespoons salt
4 garlic cloves, thinly sliced
1 shallot, minced
3 ounces Filippo Berio olive oil
1 pound strozzapreti pasta*

For the pasta: In a pasta pot, fill with half water and half red wine. Remember to always salt the water for pasta. Add the pasta when the water begins to boil. Cook the pasta until it's al dente (or for about 10 to 12 minutes). Strain, but keep warm. Be sure to add just a bit of olive oil over the pasta to ensure it does not stick. This will also add a good flavor to the dish. Spread the hot pasta over an oiled sheet tray so that it cools evenly.

For the sauce: In a thick sauté pan, add the olive oil on medium heat. Add the sliced garlic and shallot. Cook them until they're light brown. At the same time, add the basil. Be careful: It might pop when it hits the oil. Add the pork, veal and beef. Sauté them until they're fully cooked. Deglaze the pan with the red wine. Add the cream and the truffle peelings. Cook down by half or until the cream starts to form thick bubbles. Stir in the grated cheese for 2 minutes. Remove the sauce from the heat to put it in a stainless steel bowl. Add the pasta, truffle oil and the mascarpone cheese. Mix well. Let the pasta sit in the cream for 3 minutes before serving.

***Chef's note:** Strozzapreti is an imported pasta shape from Italy. It's a long, thin tube made from a square sheet of pasta that has been hand-rolled. It's available in better Italian specialty stores. If you are unable to find it, just use your favorite tube-shaped pasta. With these particular recipes, I find the thicker the sauté pan, the better. When you cook with a fondue or a cream base, a thicker pot will prevent the cheese from burning at the pan's bottom.

Serves 4.

Recommended wine:
Batasiolo Barbaresco 2000 Red (Piedmont, Italy)

Risotto with Wild Mushrooms and Peas

3 cups fresh vegetable stock
1 cup dry white wine
3 tablespoons Filippo Berio olive oil
1 cup Arborio rice
1 small onion, diced
1 cup wild mushrooms, chopped
¾ cup fresh or frozen peas
⅓ cup Parmigiano-Reggiano cheese, grated
¼ cup parsley, chopped
3 large sage leaves, chopped
salt and pepper to taste

For the risotto: In a medium-sized heavy pot, heat the olive oil over medium heat. Sauté the onion until it's translucent. Add the rice. Combine. At the same time in a separate pot, heat the stock and wine. When the stock is warmed, slowly add it to the rice, stirring constantly. Rice is done when tender but still firm to the bite (about 15 to 20 minutes).

For the vegetables: Heat an additional tablespoon of olive oil in a medium sauté pan. Add the peas and the mushrooms. Sauté them until tender. Stir them into the risotto with the parsley, sage and cheese. Mix well. Add some additional stock if too dry. Remove the pan from the heat. Adjust the seasoning with salt and pepper.

Serves 2 as a main course; 4 as a side dish.

Eggplant Rollantini

6 large eggs, beaten
4 cups fresh breadcrumbs (unseasoned)
3 cups Parmigiano-Reggiano cheese
2 large eggplants, sliced lengthwise and one-fourth of an inch thick
3 cups whole-milk mozzarella, grated
2 cups whole milk ricotta
¾ cups fresh basil, chopped
⅛ cup fresh oregano, chopped
¼ cup fresh parsley, chopped
fresh-made marinara sauce
all-purpose flour for dredging

For the eggplant: Spray 3 baking sheets with nonstick spray. Place the flour in one bowl, the eggs in another bowl and the breadcrumbs mixed with 1 cup of Parmigiano-Reggiano in a third bowl. Season the flour with salt and pepper. Coat each slice of eggplant with flour. Dredge them in the egg and then into the breadcrumbs. Arrange the eggplant on baking sheets. Bake them in a preheated 350 degree oven until golden on both sides. Remove them from the oven to cool.

For the filling: Mix the remaining ingredients — except for the sauce. Blend well. Spread the filling onto each slice of eggplant, using about 3 tablespoons per slice. Starting at the narrow end, loosely roll up the slices. Arrange them in a baking dish with the seam-side down. Spoon the marinara over the eggplant. Spread a little grated mozzarella and Parmigiano-Reggiano over the sauce. Bake in a preheated 350 degree oven for 30 minutes or until the filling has melted.

Serves 6.

Rigatoni with Italian Sausage and Broccoli Rabe

4 tablespoons Filippo Berio olive oil
3 sweet Italian sausages
3 hot Italian sausages
1 pound broccoli rabe, stems removed
4 garlic cloves, sliced
1 cup chicken stock
½ cup dry white wine
¼ cup Parmigiano-Reggiano cheese
1 pound rigatoni
kosher salt and red pepper flakes to taste

For the sausage and broccoli rabe: In a large, heavy skillet, heat the oil over medium heat. Add the garlic. Slightly brown it. Add the sausages. Brown them well. Remove them from the pan. Add the broccoli rabe to the pan. Deglaze with the white wine. Add the chicken stock. Cover the pan. Cook until the rabe is tender (about 10 minutes). Return the sausages to the pan. Remove the pan from the heat. Season with salt and red pepper flakes, but keep the sausages warm until the pasta is done.

For the pasta: In a large pot, bring salted water to a rapid boil. Add the pasta. Cook until al dente (about 10 minutes). Drain the pasta. Pour the pasta in the pan with the sausages and the rabe. Toss well. Add the grated cheese. Serve immediately.

Serves 4.

Pasta with Tuna Salsa Cruda

8 ounces marinated artichoke hearts
¼ cup capers, drained
½ cup green olives, pitted and chopped
juice and zest from 1 lemon
12 ounces fresh tuna steak, cooked to medium
½ cup Filippo Berio olive oil
kosher salt and black pepper to taste
½ cup Italian parsley, chopped
¼ cup basil, sliced
1 pound small pasta shells

For the salsa cruda: In a large bowl, mix all the ingredients together — except the pasta. Mix well. Keep the salsa cool until ready to use.

For the pasta: In a large pot, bring salted water to a boil. Cook the pasta to al dente. Drain the pasta before pouring it into a large bowl. Add the salsa cruda. Toss to coat the pasta well. Serve immediately.

Serves 4.

Seafood

Pesce e Piselli

7 ounces Chilean sea bass fillets, skin off
1 cup green peas
1 tablespoon Filippo Berio olive oil
½ ounce black truffles
2 tablespoons white truffle oil
1 sweet potato, sliced paper-thin and lengthwise
3 ounces pitted Gaeta olives
3 garlic cloves, roasted
½ cup Japanese breadcrumbs (Panko)
3 tablespoons high-fat butter
flavored oils for garnish
salt and pepper to taste

For the bass: Form the Chilean sea bass into a perfect square. Wrap the sliced sweet potato around the fish. Let the fish sit uncovered in the refrigerator for 2 hours. This allows the potato to adhere to the fish. After the fish has been refrigerated, lightly oil a baking sheet. Place it in a 350 degree oven — with tin foil wrapped around the entire plate — for about 15 minutes. Uncover. Place it back in the oven for another 5 minutes. Keep the fish warm until ready to plate.

For the pea compote: Put the peas (I like fresh peas myself, but you can use frozen peas; just let them thaw) in a food processor on low speed. Add the roasted garlic. Add salt and pepper to taste. Continue to let the mixture blend for 15 minutes so that it becomes fluffy. Add the breadcrumbs. Continue to blend for another 5 minutes. At the last minute of blending, add the truffle oil.

For the truffle butter sauce: In a skillet on medium heat, simmer the butter and the black truffles. Before the butter turns brown, take the sauce off the heat to whisk it vigorously. Reserve the sauce for plating.

For the plate: Place a spoonful of peas directly in the plate's center. Place the sea bass over the peas. Pour the truffle oil over the fish. Garnish the plate with flavored oils — such as chive oil or red pepper oil — to add more color and flavor.

Recommended wines:
Andre Brunel Chateauneuf-Du-Pape Les Cailloux Blanc 2001
Lucien Albrecht Cuvee Henri 2000 (Alsace, France)

Thumbtack Vegetables and Langoustine Froth

1 zucchini
1 yellow squash
1 large carrot
1 portobello mushroom
1 purple Japanese eggplant

For the vegetables: Wash all the vegetables thoroughly. With a 10-millimeter parisienne scoop, begin to make rounds into the whole vegetables. Sauté the vegetables in equal parts of butter, shallots and white wine. Reduce until all the liquid is "au sec" (dry).

For the froth:
4 langoustines
1 quart heavy cream, 40 percent
1 tablespoon salt
1 tablespoon butter

Cut the langoustines into small pieces. In a large, heavy pot, add the butter on medium heat. Sauté the shallots and langoustine until they start to caramelize very lightly. Add the cream. Reduce by half. Remove the pot from the heat. Strain the mixture through a China cap three times. With a handheld immersion blender, create a froth by blending on high speed. When the froth is light and airy, spoon it onto the cooked thumbtack vegetables Serve immediately.

Grilled Coho Salmon with Potato Gnocchi and Tomato Reduction

1 8-ounce Coho salmon fillet (substitute farm-raised if out of season)
½ teaspoon dry grape rinds · 2 tablespoon grape seed oil
salt and pepper to taste
1½-pounds fresh tomatoes, peeled, seeded, drained and chopped
1 shallot · ¼ pound truffle butter · 1 quart white wine

For the bouquet garni
(the following herbs wrapped in cheesecloth and then tied):
4 parsley sprigs · 2 bay leaves
1 fresh thyme sprig · 4 garlic cloves
1 quart tomato juice · juice from one cucumber
8 ounces potato gnocchi · 1 tablespoon salt

For the salmon: Rub the salmon fillet with the grape seed oil, being sure to cover both sides. Season the salmon on both sides with salt and pepper. Grill both sides on a hot grill to achieve grill marks. Remove the salmon from the grill. Finish it off in a 350 degree oven for 8 to 10 minutes.

For the tomato reduction: In a heavy saucepan, add oil to sauté the shallots and the garlic until brown. Add the wine. Reduce by half. Pour the pot's contents into a separate bowl. Put the shallot, oil and onion mixture in a blender to puree. Add the onion mixture to the recipe only at the end. If it's added and pureed at the same time, it will make the sauce turn orange. In the same pot, add all the remaining ingredients. Bring them to a simmer. Take out the bouquet garni. With a handheld immersion mixer, puree all the ingredients until smooth. Add the onion mixture. Continue to simmer by half until the reduction has a full body or is thick enough to coat a spoon's back. Strain through a China cap. Set the sauce aside.

For the gnocchi: In a pasta pot with boiling, salted water, add the gnocchi. Cook until they're al dente. Strain from the water. In a sauté pan, heat 2 tablespoons of butter and 1 tablespoon of olive oil. When very hot, add the gnocchi. Brown well. Keep warm until ready to plate.

For the plate: In a wide-brimmed, deep plate, place the grilled salmon in the center. Pool the tomato reduction around the salmon. Place the gnocchi around the salmon in the reduction. Garnish the top of the salmon with fresh thyme.

Recommended wines:
Chateau Chassagne Montrachet St Aubain "Les Chermors" (Burgundy, France)
Little Penguin Shiraz (Southwest Australia)

Asian Sea Bass Steamed in Cabbage Leaves

2 pounds black sea bass fillets or striped bass fillets
2 teaspoons red chili paste
1 tablespoon fresh lemon juice
2 teaspoons fresh ginger, grated
1 teaspoon garlic, minced
2 teaspoons soy sauce
1 head napa or savoy cabbage
4 scallions, chopped
1 teaspoon white sesame seeds
1 teaspoon black sesame seeds
3 teaspoons sesame oil
1 red pepper, julienned
1 green pepper, julienned
½-pound snow or snap peas

For the bass: Cut the bass into 4-ounce pieces. Mix the chili paste, lemon juice, ginger, garlic and soy sauce together. Pour over the bass. Toss. Marinate for 2 hours.

For the cabbage leaves: Remove the cabbage's core. Remove its outer leaves carefully, as these are what will be used to wrap the bass. Blanch the leaves in salted water for 3 minutes and then place them in an ice-water bath. Dry the leaves when cool. Break the hard stem on the leaf so that it can lie flat. Overlap several leaves. Place a piece of bass toward the leaves' bottom. Place some red and green pepper strips and snow peas on the bass. Sprinkle both colors of sesame seeds and the scallions on top. Fold the leaves together. Roll the leaves away from you to completely cover the bass. Make the roll as tight as possible. Repeat this process until all the bass is used. Place the bass in a steamer for 10 to 15 minutes.

For the plate: Cut each roll crosswise into 4 or 5 slices. Arrange on the plate so that the bass and the vegetables are visible. Pour sesame oil lightly over each piece. Serve with steamed rice.

Serves 4 to 6.

Recommended wines:
Pinot Blanc Byron Vineyards 1999 (Santa Maria Valley, California, USA)
Marsanne McDowell Vineyards 2001 (Mendocino County, California, USA)

Snake River Trout with Andouille Shrimp Stuffing

6 ounces butter
1 onion, diced
1 carrot, diced
1 celery stalk, diced
8 ounces shrimp, peeled, cleaned and chopped
8 ounces Andouille sausage, diced
8 ounces breadcrumbs
8 ounces chicken stock
4 pan-dressed Idaho trout
1 tablespoon fresh thyme
½ pint cherry tomatoes

For the stuffing: For this stuffing, the ingredients should be medium-diced. You really want to see the vegetables, shrimp and great sausage. In a heavy-bottom saucepan, melt the butter to sweat the onions until they're translucent. Add the sausage. Cook it until it's brown. Add onions and carrots. In three parts, add the chicken stock, bring it to a boil and then reduce it. Add diced bread, shrimp and thyme. Thicken the mixture with breadcrumbs. Spread it on a sheet pan to cool.

For the trout: Lay the fish open skin-side down. Spoon 8 ounces of stuffing onto each fish. Fold the fish over so that they look like a fish again. Place them on a roasting pan. Put them in an oven at 350 degrees for 15 to 20 minutes.

For the dish: The best way to serve the fish is family-style. In a sauté pan, heat more stuffing. Place the stuffing at the platter's bottom. Place the fish in the stuffing, alternating the direction each fish faces. The fish should look as if they are swimming. Be sure to have extra stuffing hot, as your guests will not be able to stop themselves.

For the garnish: Roast some cherry tomatoes with whole thyme sprigs. Surround the platter. The vibrant colors should bring the dish to life.

Recommended wines:
Chryseia Prats & Symington Douro 2000 Red (Portugal)
Lusco Albarino 2003 White (Rias Baixas, Spain)

Soft-Shell Crabs

1 dozen soft-shell blue crabs, jumbo or whale size
1 quart buttermilk
2 cups unbleached white flour
1 cup whole wheat flour
1½ cups coarsely ground yellow cornmeal
½ cup plain breadcrumbs
2 tablespoons crab seasoning
1 tablespoon kosher salt
2 teaspoons baking powder
½ teaspoon white pepper

To clean the crabs: Crabs should be alive when you purchase them. To clean them, use a kitchen shear to cut the face off, making sure to remove the eyes and the mouth. Squeeze the head to remove the sack behind the eyes. Flip the crab over, and with a knife, pull the apron up to lift the top shell up but not off the body. Remove the lungs, which are yellow and fingerlike in appearance. If you are unsure about doing this, ask your fishmonger to clean the crabs when you purchase them. Once clean, place the crabs in a bowl. Pour the buttermilk over them, making sure the crabs are completely covered. Salt and pepper lightly. Cover them to refrigerate for 2 to 3 hours.

For the breading: Pour all remaining ingredients into a flour sifter to mix well. Remove the crabs from the refrigerator. Shake off the excess buttermilk. Dredge the crabs one at a time in the breading mixture. Shake off the excess. Place them on a wire rack until ready to cook.

To fry the crabs: Heat a large cast-iron skillet on the stovetop. Pour peanut oil into the pan. Use enough oil so that it comes about halfway up the pan's sides. Carefully place the crabs one at a time — top-shell down — in the hot oil. Stand back, as the crabs will splatter oil as they start to cook. Carefully turn the crabs over to brown the bottom shell. The crabs are done when they have an even golden color. Remove them from the oil. Drain the crabs on brown paper to remove excess oil.

For the plate: Arrange the crabs on a plate. They are best served hot and with tartar sauce, hot sauce or malt vinegar. They can also be served on a roll with coleslaw for a real Southern treat.

Recommended wines:
Kenwood Russian River Pinot Noir 2001 Red (Sonoma, California, USA)
Wolf Blass Shiraz 2001 Red (South Australia)

Prosciutto-Wrapped Tuna

2 8-ounce pieces ahi tuna
3 ounces prosciutto di Parma, thinly sliced
2 peeled chef potatoes, diced into 1-inch cubes
10 ounces celery root, peeled and diced into 1-inch pieces
1 pound Parmigiano-Reggiano cheese, grated
1 teaspoon truffle oil · 2 pieces baby leeks
2 pieces baby bok choy · 2 baby carrots
2 pearl onions · butcher's twine
1 teaspoon tangerine oil

For the tuna: On a flat surface, lay the prosciutto out, overlapping each piece but not covering them completely. Cut the tuna so that it will measure 2 inches by 6 inches to resemble a brick. Place the tuna on the prosciutto. Wrap the tuna. Use butcher's twine to tie the tuna to secure the meat on the fish. In a hot pan, add 1 teaspoon oil, sear each tuna for 45 to 60 seconds on each side and then remove it from the heat. Remove the string, but keep the tuna warm.

For the potato and celery root puree: Place the potatoes in a medium pot filled with salted water. Bring the water to a boil. Cook the potatoes until their tender. Strain. Set aside. Repeat the process with the celery root. In a food processor, combine the hot potatoes and celery root. Puree them for 8 to 10 minutes with the cheese until blended smooth. (It will have a shine to it when it's ready.)

For the vegetables: In a 3-quart pot, boil water. Clean all the baby vegetables. Poach them separately. Chill them in ice water right away. In a pan, add 1 teaspoon butter to toss all the cooked vegetables.

For the plate: Slice a small piece off the tuna's end to show the rare meat. On a large plate, pipe the potato and celery root puree in the center. Place the small piece of tuna in the puree. Place the larger piece over it. Lay the baby vegetables around the tuna in an artistic design.

Chef's note: I prefer to serve (and eat!) tuna very rare, especially sushi-quality ahi. If you do not like your fish this rare, the tuna will need a longer cooking time than recommended above. After searing the tuna, place them in a preheated 350 degree oven. Cook them to the desired doneness. About 10 minutes will achieve well done.

Recommended wines:
Chateau St. Jean Merlot 2000 (Sonoma, California, USA)
McDowell Vineyards Grenache Rose 2000 (Mendocino County, California, USA)

Grandma's Belgian Mussels

1 bag (10 pounds) Prince Edward Island mussels, beards removed
1 fennel bulb, tops removed and cut into thin strips
2 leeks, greens only and chopped
2 shallots, minced
¼ pound unsalted butter, cut into pieces
¼ cup Filippo Berio olive oil
¼ cup Molinari sambuca
2 bottles (750 milliliters) dark Belgian beer
salt and pepper to taste

To start: Cut all the vegetables. Make sure the leeks are clean, as they are often covered in mud. Cut the leeks. Let them stand in cold water. Drain them. Cover them with water again until they're clean. Heat a large pot on medium heat. Melt butter. Add olive oil. When hot, add all the vegetables. Sauté them until they're soft, browning slightly.

For the mussels: Clean the mussels in cold water to remove any sand. To de-beard them, grab the beard's exposed end to pull it off. When all the mussels have been de-bearded, put them into a pot with the vegetables. Mix to coat the mussels with butter and oil. Add the sambuca. Stir. Pour the beer over the mussels. Cook them until the shells start to open.

For the plate: Remove the shells from the pot when they have all opened. Spoon the mussels into 6 soup bowls. Divide the liquid with the vegetables into the bowls. Serve with a crusty bread or baguette. Belgian beer or ale goes well with this dish. Serve it at room temperature in large, wide-mouth glasses.

Recommended wines:
Domaire De La Quilla Muscadet Sérve et Maine 2001 (Loire, France)
Martini & Rossi Prosecco (Frizante)

MOLINARI
Sambuca extra
IMPORTED

Blue Point Oysters in Molinari Sambuca with Leek Fondue

2 bunches leeks, cleaned, diced and greens reserved
1 cup Molinari sambuca
4 ounces unsalted butter
4 ounces all-purpose flour
1 dozen Blue Point or other large East Coast oysters, shucked and reserved
1 quart heavy cream
salt and pepper to taste

For the oysters: In a heavy-bottom pot, add butter. When melted, add the leek whites, coating them with the fat. Do not overcook. Add the flour. Cook for 3 to 5 minutes, stirring constantly. Deglaze with the sambuca. Add the cream. Bring the mixture to a boil. Lower the heat to a simmer. Reduce the fondue by half or until very thick. Chill in the refrigerator until completely cool. The fondue should be extremely thick. When ready to use, cover the entire top of the oysters with the fondue. Bake at 425 degrees for 15 minutes.

For the dish: As a butlered hors d'oeuvre, 1 oyster is sufficient; as an appetizer, 3 oysters are generally a good serving size.

For the garnish: Resting the oysters in coarse sea salt will prevent them from sliding around the plate. Julienne the leek tops. Fry them until they're crispy. Season with salt and pepper. Sprinkle the garnish on the oysters. This will add a crisp texture and a good color.

Seafood Paella

½ cup short grain rice · 10 saffron threads
2 shallots, peeled and diced
3 ounces dried chorizo
2 ounces Filippo Berio olive oil
1 fresh thyme sprig
8 cockle clams, washed well
5 large New Zealand green mussels
4 U-12 shrimp, peeled and de-veined (with tail intact)
2 plum tomatoes, seeded and diced
1 6-ounce airline chicken breast, boneless, skin on and with wing drum attached
2 teaspoons Filippo Berio olive oil
¼ teaspoon fennel pollen (optional)
1 piquillo pepper, roasted (optional)
1 tablespoon chives, minced
salt and cracked black pepper to taste

For the airline chicken: In a skillet on high heat, add the 2 tablespoons of oil. Heat it until it's smoking. Season the chicken with salt and pepper on both sides. Place the chicken skin-side down for about 3 minutes or until the skin is completely golden brown and crispy. Flip the chicken over. Place it in a 375 degree oven for 15 minutes. Keep warm.

For the rice: In a heavy-bottom 1-quart saucepan, bring 1⅔ cup of water to a boil. Add salt and saffron to taste. Wait until the water has turned yellow before adding the rice. Add the rice, stirring well to avoid sticking. Once the rice has returned to a boil, reduce the heat to a very low simmer. Cover the pot. Let the rice cook for 25 minutes.

For the paella: In a medium saucepan, add 2 ounces of olive oil. Heat it until it's smoking. Add the shallots and chorizo. Cook until golden brown and the oil's color has turned red. Add the fresh thyme, cockles, mussels and shrimp. Continue to cook for 4 minutes. Add the wine. Reduce by half. Add the diced tomatoes, fennel pollen and the rice. Continue to cook for about 2 minutes. Add the chives at the very end. Mix the rice and the seafood around in the pot with a wooden spoon. If needed, adjust the seasoning with salt and pepper.

For the plate: I like to serve the dish in a cast-iron skillet — just for presentation purposes. Put the airline chicken breast and the piquillo pepper on top of the rice to enjoy a taste of Spain.

Recommended wines:
Beringer Napa Valley Sauvignon Blanc 2002 (Napa Valley, California, USA)
Kim Crawford Sauvignon Blanc 2003 (Marlborough, New Zealand)

Shrimp Gabriella

9 U-10 shrimp, peeled and de-veined
2 shallots, diced
1 cup brandy
1 cup seasoned breadcrumbs
2 cups chicken stock
2 garlic cloves
1 cup fresh tomatoes, diced, seeds removed and drained
6 fresh basil leaves
2 tablespoons good-quality balsamic vinegar (aged balsamic preferred)
1 cup rice (any rice can be used, but be creative)
1 cup Parmigiano-Reggiano
1 ounce crème fraiche
1 bunch fresh sage
1 ounce fresh black truffles, sliced (use canned truffles if fresh is unavailable)
2 ounces Filippo Berio olive oil
1 ounce white truffle oil

For the rice: Use any short-grain rice you like. In a medium, heavy saucepan, add the rice to the chicken stock in a 2:1 ratio (2 parts water to 1 part rice). Simmer on low for about 20 to 25 minutes.

For the Gabriella: In a hot sauté pan, brown the shallots, garlic and fresh sage in oil. Add the shrimp, season with salt and pepper and then continue to let the mixture cook in the oil for 5 minutes. Deglaze with brandy, removing the pan from the heat first. Put the pan back on the heat. Be careful, as it will ignite. When the heat burns out, add a half-cup of chicken stock and 1 cup of white sweet wine. Add fresh basil, seasoned breadcrumbs and diced tomatoes. Continue to cook for about another 10 minutes. If it gets too thick from the breadcrumbs, thin it out with more stock. At the very end of cooking, add shaved black truffles. Drizzle the truffle oil over the dish. Happy eating!

Recommended wines:
Domaine Drouhim Chardonnay 2002 White (Oregon)
Bedell Viognier 2003 White (North Fork, Long Island, New York, USA)

Organic Salmon with Chorizo

7 ounces organic white salmon fillets
1 pint cherry tomatoes, stems removed
3 teaspoons Filippo Berio olive oil
1 tablespoon good-quality or aged balsamic vinegar
1 marinated artichoke heart, roughly chopped
3 tablespoons Filippo Berio olive oil
3 shallots, thinly sliced
½ cup white wine
1 fresh thyme sprig
1 pinch fennel pollen (available in specialty stores or online from a spice company)
¼ cup apple juice
salt and freshly cracked black pepper to taste

For the salmon: Season both sides of the salmon with salt and pepper. In a sauté pan on high, heat the oil until it smokes. Place the salmon flesh-side down in the pan, moving it slightly to avoid sticking. Continue to cook in the pan for 3 minutes on each side. Deglaze with apple juice. Reduce by one-third. Slice the chorizo paper-thin into half-moon shapes. Place the chorizo on top of the salmon to resemble scales. The heat from the salmon will warm the chorizo. Set aside until plating.

For the sauce: In a 1-quart saucepan on high heat, add the oil and shallots. Continue to cook until brown. Deglaze with white wine. Reduce by one-third. Add the cherry tomatoes. Continue to cook the sauce down until it thickens. Add the artichokes into the sauce. Continue to simmer. Taste for salt and pepper. Pull the pot off the heat.

For the plate: In a 12-inch white dish, add the cherry tomato sauce and then mirror the plate's inside. Place the salmon with the chorizo scales in the center. Sprinkle a little fennel pollen on top of the chorizo. Drizzle a bit of aged balsamic vinegar around the plate's sides.

Recommended wines:
Bonterra Syrah Red (Mendocino, California, USA)
Louis Jadot Saint-Veron Domaine Aux Loupe 2002 White (Burgundy, France)

Salmon Poached with Vinegar

4 8-ounce pieces of Icelandic Naturally Salmon (filleted and pin boned out)
2 carrots, chopped
2 shallots, chopped
2 stalks of celery, chopped
1 sprig of fresh thyme
1 tablespoon of rice wine vinegar
2 tablespoons of Molinari Sambuca
½ sweet white wine
1 ½ pound of baby spinach
3 tablespoons of salted butter
1 pinch of Bob's Red Mill Lemon and Pepper Spice
Touch of Filippo Berio Extra Virgin olive oil

For the salmon: Place the fish in a large sauce pan with the carrots, celery, shallots; add the vinegar and sufficient water to completely cover the fish. Add the fresh thyme and make sure that it is soaked into the liquid. Add the wine and the Molinari Sambuca and bring to a boil. Reduce the heat and bring to a simmer for 12 minutes.

For the spinach: When there are four minutes of cooking time remaining place the spinach on top so that the steam from the water cooks the leaves. Drain, cool, and press out excess liquid with a strainer. Chop it coarsely and sauté it for a few minutes in olive oil.

For the plate: Remover the spinach and place on a serving platter. Arrange the fish over the top of the spinach Melt the butter and pour over the salmon. Spinkle the lemon pepper spice on top of the dish.

Seared Scallops with Mushroom Marmalade

1 pound sea scallops, U-10 size, dry-packed preferably and side muscle removed
2 teaspoons Filippo Berio olive oil
½ cup porcini mushrooms
½ cup sherry vinegar
1 cup veal demi-glaze
¼ cup prune juice
salt and cracked black pepper

For the scallops: In a cast-iron pan on high heat, add the oil until it smokes. Pat the cleaned scallops dry on both sides. Season them with salt and pepper. Be sure to remove the small side muscle, as it's very tough. Place the scallops in the pan. Sear them on both sides until they turn golden brown. Usually, the cooking process will be 30 seconds on each side. Remove them from the pan, but keep them warm until ready to plate.

For the mushroom marmalade: In a 1-quart saucepan, sauté the shallots and mushrooms until golden brown. Deglaze with sherry vinegar. Add the prune juice. Reduce by half. Add the demi-glaze. Reduce until thick and bubbling. This is a sign that the sauce is ready. Adjust the seasoning with salt and pepper.

For the plate: On a 10½-inch dish, spoon the mushroom marmalade in the center. Directly on top, place the seared scallops. Add some sauce around the plate. Enjoy!

This recipe must give credit to Chef James Mauir.

Recommended wines:
Hogue Pinot Gris 2001 White
Marcel Deiss Riesling Beblenheim 2002 (Alsace, France)

Seared Trout with Tomato Water

2 4-ounce trout fillets
2 red plum tomatoes, poached, seeded and skinned
2 yellow plum tomatoes, poached, seeded and skinned
2 green tomatoes, poached, seeded and skinned
1 fresh oregano sprig
5 pounds beefsteak tomatoes, cut into large pieces
2 ounces red and yellow sun-dried tomatoes, julienned
8 ounces tomato juice (optional)
2 slices brioche bread (one-fourth of an inch thick, cut into a 4-inch by 4-inch squares, cut into four and then each one cut in half to form a triangle; dredge with clarified butter; and then toast the pieces)
3 ounces cashew butter · white pepper to taste
ground sea salt to taste · 5 large coffee filters
½ cup tri-colored Israeli couscous · 1 cup water · 3 ounces goat cheese

For the couscous: In a 1-quart pot, boil the water. Add the couscous. Lower the heat to medium. Continue to cook for 4 minutes. Strain the couscous, mix with 3 ounces of goat cheese and then set the couscous aside.

For the tomato water: Line 5 large coffee filters on the inside of a large strainer. Pour the cut beefsteak tomatoes into the coffee filters, smash the tomatoes and then let them strain for 24 hours. The result should be a clear water-like substance with a very strong tomato flavor.

For the fish: Put a nonstick sauté pan on the stovetop at medium heat. Add grape seed oil. Heat it until it smokes. Season the fish with salt and white pepper. Place the fish in the pan, cook 1 minute on each side and then remove it from the pan. In a separate, deep casserole dish, rest the fish in half the tomato water. When the fish is ready to be served, put the casserole in a preheated oven at 350 degrees for 3 minutes.

For the tomatoes: In a 1-quart saucepan, pour in the tomato water. Bring up the temperature to 100 degrees. Cut the poached tomatoes in half. Put them in a small hand-strainer. Leave them in the tomato water for 5 minutes.

For the brioche: Spread the cashew butter between the bread. Close the two sides.

For the plate: Scoop 3 ounces of tri-colored couscous into the plate's center. Take the trout from the tomato water. Place it on top of the couscous. Strain the poached, skinned and seeded tomatoes. Place them on top of the fish. Peel oregano buds. Place them on top of the tomatoes. Place the brioche with the cashew butter on the fish's side. Use the tomato juice as a dipping condiment for the brioche (optional). Happy eating!

Recommended wines:
Yarden Katzrin Chardonnay 2000 White (Golan Heights, Israel)
Domaine Houchort Cotes de Provence Rose (Provence, France)

Phillips Crab Cake

1 pound Phillips crabmeat
1 egg
2 teaspoon Worcestershire sauce
¼ teaspoon dry mustard
2 tablespoon mayonnaise
1 teaspoon lemon juice
1 tablespoon mustard
1 tablespoon melted butter
1 teaspoon parsley flakes
1 teaspoon Phillips seafood seasoning
½ cup breadcrumbs

Compliments of Phillips: In a large mixing bowl, combine all the ingredients — except for the crabmeat. Gently fold in the crabmeat, being careful not to break up the lumps. Shape it into cakes. Pan fry or bake at 375 degrees for 12 to 15 minutes or until evenly brown on each side and the cakes reach an internal temperature of 165 degrees.

Chef's note: I have tried many crab cake recipes over the years. This is by far the simplest and the best. As a little twist, try serving these for your next cocktail party as an hors d'oeuvre. Before cooking, shape the crab as small bite-size cakes. Serve them with a fruit salsa.

Recommended wines:
Mommessin Brouilly 2002 Red (Beaujolais, France)
Michel Picard Vouvray (Loine, France)

Planked and Roasted Striped Bass with Lobster Roll Stuffing

1 whole striped bass (8 to 10 pounds) gutted, scaled and with head and tail on
1½ pounds lobster meat
3 celery ribs, finely chopped
1 small onion, finely diced
1½ cups mayonnaise
salt and pepper to taste
½ cup Filippo Berio olive oil
1 organic cedar plank about 2 feet long, available at gourmet or grill stores

For the stuffing: Run your hand through the lobster meat to make sure all the cartilage is removed. Add celery, onion and mayonnaise. Mix well. Season with salt and pepper. Set aside.

For the fish: Your fishmonger can gut and clean the fish for you. When ready to use, rinse the belly cavity out with water. Dry well. Fill the cavity with stuffing. Before placing the stuffed fish on the cedar plank, rub both sides with olive oil. Cover loosely with aluminum foil. Place in a preheated gas grill's center. Lower the heat to medium. Cook approximately 8 minutes per pound or until the meat is opaque.

For the plate: For a dramatic effect, present the fish to the table on the plank. Remove the skin from the top of the fish, and with 2 forks, remove the top layer of fish. Remove the stuffing. Flip the fish over to remove the bottom layer. If done correctly, all the bones should remain on the plank.

Serves 6 to 8.

Recommended wines:
Robert Monclavi Napa Fumme Blanc 2002 White (Napa Valley, California, USA)
Edna Valley Pinot Gris 2000 (San Louis Obispo, California, USA)

Seared Medallions of Monkfish with Blood Orange Basil Cream

2 large monkfish fillets, cut into 6-ounce pieces
8 blood oranges
2 cups heavy cream
1 cup crème fraiche
6 large basil leaves, cut into strips
½ cup Filippo Berio olive oil
salt and pepper to taste

For the sauce: Squeeze the juice from 6 oranges into a small bowl. In a heavy saucepan, bring the heavy cream to a boil. Reduce by half. Add the orange juice. Mix thoroughly. Reduce the heat to add the crème fraiche. Stir to thicken the sauce. Remove the saucepan from the heat to add the basil. Keep the sauce warm until the fish is cooked.

For the monkfish: Remove any skin or membrane left on the fillets. Season both sides with salt and pepper. Heat the sauté pan with olive oil. Place the fish into the hot pan. Sear both sides. Remove the fish from the pan, put them in a shallow roasting pan and then place them in a preheated oven at 350 degrees. Cook until the fish is firm to the touch (about 10 minutes). Remove the fish from the oven.

For the plate: Cut segments from the two remaining blood oranges. Remove the skin and any membrane. Place the fish in the plate's center. Spoon the blood orange cream around the fish. Place several orange segments in the cream around the fish. Place a whole basil leaf on the fish before serving.

Serves 4 to 6.

Recommended wine:
Cloudy Bay Sauvignon Blanc 2002 White (New Zealand)

Recommended mixed drink:

Blood Orange Martini:

2 ounces Skyy orange vodka
½ ounce blood orange juice
½ ounce Tuaca

Fill it into a cocktail shaker on ice. Strain the drink into a martini glass.

Pasta with Smoked Salmon and Dill Sauce

1 pound pasta, rigatoni or other tube-shaped pasta
1 pound pencil asparagus, ends trimmed and cut diagonally into 2-inch pieces
1 shallot, minced
1 tablespoon unsalted butter
¼ cup brandy
1 cup heavy cream
2 teaspoons fresh lemon zest
¼ cup dill, freshly chopped
¼ pound pepper-crusted smoked salmon, sliced and cut into thin strips
salt and pepper to taste

For the sauce: In a heavy saucepan, melt the butter on medium heat. When hot, add the shallot. Sauté until limp. Remove the saucepan from the heat. Add the brandy. Be careful, as the brandy will flame. Return the saucepan to the stove. Add the heavy cream and the zest. Reduce by one-third, add the salmon and then remove the saucepan from the heat.

For the pasta: In a heavy pot, bring 8 quarts of salted water to a boil. Add the pasta. Cook for 4 minutes. Add the asparagus to the pot. Cook until the pasta and asparagus are al dente. Drain. Pour the pasta into a large bowl. Toss it with the dill and the sauce. Crack fresh ground pepper over the top. Serve immediately.

Serves 4.

Pan-Fried Trout with Pancetta

4 slices pancetta
5 tablespoons butter
2 whole 10- to 12-ounce trout, bones removed
all-purpose flour for dredging
1 cup scallions, thinly sliced
4 tablespoons fresh lemon juice
½ cup dry white wine
4 teaspoons capers
2 teaspoons tarragon, freshly chopped
salt and pepper to taste

For the trout: Cook the pancetta in a large skillet on medium heat until crisp. Drain it on a paper towel. Pour most of the drippings from the pan. Melt 1 tablespoon of butter in the pan. Season the flour with salt and pepper. Dredge the trout in the seasoned flour. Shake off the excess. Place the fish in the pan. Brown them for about 3 minutes. Turn the fish over to brown well. Cook until the fish is opaque. Remove them from the pan.

For the sauce: Slice the bacon into thin pieces. Pour off all the drippings from the pan. Add the remaining butter to the pan. Add the scallions to the pan. Cook for 2 minutes. Add the bacon, white wine, lemon juice, capers and tarragon. Season with salt and pepper, reduce slightly and then pour the sauce over the fish. Serve immediately.

Serves 2.

Grilled Wild Salmon with Red Pepper Corn Salsa

4 red bell peppers, seeded, cored and diced
4 tablespoons Filippo Berio olive oil
4 cups fresh corn, cut from 5 ears
3 garlic cloves, minced
2 tablespoons cilantro, chopped
2 tablespoons fresh lemon juice
2 tablespoons fresh lime juice
1 tablespoon jalapeño pepper, seeded and minced
10 6-ounce skinless wild salmon fillets (if unavailable, use farm-raised salmon)
¼ cup lemon juice
¼ cup Filippo Berio olive oil
2 tablespoons honey
1 tablespoon cumin
kosher salt and pepper to taste

For the salsa: In a large cast-iron pan, heat the 4 tablespoons of oil over medium heat. Add the garlic and jalapeño pepper. Sauté them. Add the peppers and the corn. Cook until the corn browns slightly. Add the lemon juice, lime juice and cilantro. Toss well. Remove the salsa from the heat. Reserve.

For the salmon: Season both sides of the fish with salt and pepper. In a bowl, mix the remaining ingredients together. Place the fish in a shallow pan. Pour the marinade over them. Refrigerate for 30 minutes, turning the salmon once. On a hot grill, place the salmon skin-side up. Cook for 5 to 6 minutes. Turn the fish. Cook for an additional 5 to 6 minutes. The salmon should be opaque in the center. Remove them from the grill.

For the table: Place the salmon on a platter. Pour the salsa over the fish. Serve family-style.

Serves 10.

Oysters Rockefeller

1 garlic clove
2 cups fresh spinach
½ cup scallions, chopped
1½ sticks unsalted butter, at room temperature
½ cup breadcrumbs
6 bacon strips, cooked
2 tablespoons Molinari sambuca
1 teaspoon hot sauce
24 large oysters, shucked and with shells reserved
¼ cup Parmigiano-Reggiano cheese, freshly shredded

For the filling: In a food processor, finely chop the garlic. Add the spinach and green onions. Pulse the processor until they are medium-chopped. Add the bacon. Proceed to finely chop the mixture. Remove the filling from the processor, but reserve it in a bowl. Combine the butter, breadcrumbs, sambuca and hot sauce in the processor. Mix until well blended. Return the spinach to the bowl. Pulse until blended. Remove the filling from the processor. Chill well.

For the oysters: Arrange the oysters on a baking sheet. Place 1 tablespoon of filling on each oyster. Garnish with the shredded cheese. Bake in a preheated 450 degree oven. When the filling has browned, remove the oysters from the oven (approximately 8 to 10 minutes). Serve immediately.

Chef's note: Oysters Rockefeller can be used as a first course or as passed hors d'oeuvre for parties.

Grilled Shrimp with Tropical Fruit Salsa

2 pounds large shrimp, 16/20 size, peeled and de-veined with the tails on
5 tablespoons Filippo Berio olive oil
5 tablespoons lime juice
5 tablespoons lemon juice
1 teaspoon cumin
1 pineapple, peeled, cored and cut into half-inch-thick slices
1 large mango, peeled, pit removed and cut into half-inch chunks
1 banana, cut into thick slices
1 medium red onion, chopped
½ cup fresh cilantro, chopped
1 large jalapeño pepper, seeded and finely chopped

For the shrimp: Thread the shrimp onto several metal skewers. Mix half the olive oil, half the lemon juice, half the lime juice and the cumin together. Place the shrimp in a shallow dish. Pour the marinade over. Cover before refrigerating for a half hour. When ready to cook, grill on hot grill until the shrimp are opaque. Remove them from the grill, but keep them warm.

For the salsa: Season all the fruits with salt and pepper. Place on hot grill. Cook until the mango and the banana have browned slightly, but cook the pineapple until it's tender. Remove the fruits from the grill. Place them on a work surface. Cut the pineapple into small pieces. Place them in a mixing bowl. Add the remaining ingredients. Toss well.

For the table: Place the shrimp on a platter. Pour the salsa over. Serve immediately.

Serves 6.

Clams Oreganata

2 dozen little-neck clams, scrubbed well
1 pound kosher salt
¼ cup Filippo Berio olive oil
6 garlic cloves, thinly sliced
1½ cups Japanese breadcrumbs (Panko)
3 tablespoons oregano, freshly chopped
3 tablespoons basil, freshly chopped
kosher salt and pepper to taste
½ cup shredded Parmigiano-Reggiano cheese

To open the clams: Using a clam knife, carefully open the clams. Discard the top shell. Using the knife, loosen the clam from the bottom shell, but do not remove it. Pour any liquid into a bowl for reserve. Spread the kosher salt onto a large baking sheet. Position the clams in the salt.

For the filling: Spread the breadcrumbs out on a baking sheet. Place them in a preheated 350 degree oven. Watch the breadcrumbs so that they do not burn. Stir often to ensure even browning. Remove the breadcrumbs from oven when they're golden. In a large sauté pan, heat the olive oil on medium heat. Add the garlic. Brown it well. Add the basil and the oregano, but be careful of splatters. Add the breadcrumbs to the pan. Toss well. Season with salt and pepper before removing the mixture from the heat.

To bake the clams: Add the reserved clam juice to the filling. Place a spoonful of filling in each clam. Add a little shredded cheese to the top of each clam. Place them under a hot broiler. Cook until the cheese is melted and brown. Remove the clams from the oven. Place them on a large platter. Drizzle extra virgin olive oil over each clam before serving.

Chef's note: The clams can be served as a plated appetizer or as a passed hors d'oeuvre.

Oyster Stew

6 tablespoons Filippo Berio olive oil
4 potatoes, peeled and diced
3 shallot bulbs, peeled and diced
3 celery stalks, diced
½ onion, peeled and diced
2 carrots, diced
1 quart water
½ gallon freshly shucked oysters in liquor
1 teaspoon nutmeg
1 cup Chardonnay
1 pint heavy cream
6 tablespoons flour
½ bunch fresh thyme, leaves pulled off
salt and white pepper to taste

For the stew: In a large saucepan on high heat, add the oil. When the oil is hot, add the diced shallots and onion. Cook until translucent. Add the carrot and celery. Cook 5 to 7 minutes more. Sift the flour into the saucepan. Stir the flour into the vegetables. Deglaze with Chardonnay. Add the cream, water and potatoes. Bring to a boil. Lower to a simmer to reduce. When the potatoes are fork-tender, add the oysters. Bring the stew back to a boil. Reduce until nappe (or when the liquid coats a spoon's back). Season with salt, pepper and fresh thyme.

For the dish: Spoon the stew into a rustic bowl. Serve it with a warm, buttered sourdough roll.

For the garnish: Something spicy is needed: Roll 1 oyster in cornmeal, salt, pepper and cayenne. Flash fry. Float it in the bowl's middle. Try a drizzle of a flavorful hot sauce — but not too much. We don't want to take away from the main dish.

Poultry

Chicken Casserole with Chanterelles and White Beans

1 cup white beans, cooked
½ pound chanterelle mushrooms, cleaned
3 tablespoons Filippo Berio olive oil
½ cup chicken stock
1 cup sweet red wine
1 fresh rosemary sprig, leaves only and chopped
2 shallots, diced
1 tablespoon unsalted butter
1 cup demi-glaze
1 bay leaf
2 whole garlic cloves
1 bunch chives, minced
1 tablespoon crème fraiche
1 whole 3½-pound chicken
salted water
salt and pepper to taste

For the chicken: Wash the chicken with salted water and pat dry. Cut the chicken into 8 pieces: 2 legs, 2 wings, 2 breasts and 2 thighs. Set aside.

For the cooking: In an ovenproof pan on high heat, add the olive oil. Sear the chicken on both sides to brown well. Add the garlic, rosemary, shallots and bay leaf. Cook for 5 minutes, turning and tossing well. Place the pan into the oven on 350 degrees for 35 minutes.

For the sauce: In a saucepan, add the butter on medium heat. Add the chanterelles. Season with salt and pepper. Continue to cook for 3 minutes. Add the wine, chicken stock, cooked beans and demi-glaze. Cook for 3 more minutes. Add the sauce to the pan with the chicken. Continue to cook the chicken in the sauce for an additional 15 minutes. After that time, remove the chicken from the oven. Add the chives and the crème fraiche to the sauce. Adjust the seasoning with salt and pepper. Let it stand at room temperature for 10 minutes before serving.

Serves 4.

Recommended wines:
Qupe Marsanne (Santa Barbara County, California, USA)
Erath Pinot Noir 2001 (Oregon, USA)

Roasted Chicken — Done Right

One 3½ to 5 pound roasting chicken
2 lemons
2 fresh rosemary sprigs
2 fresh flat-leaf parsley sprigs
2 fresh thyme sprigs
3 tablespoons soft unsalted butter
2 tablespoons Filippo Berio olive oil
1 teaspoon truffle oil
salt and black pepper

For the chicken: Always clean the chicken. With your fingers, remove the kidneys and the gizzard. Rinse the cavity and the skin with fresh cold water. Rub the cavity and the chicken's outside with salt and pepper. Remove the skin from the lemons. Place lemon segments in the chicken's cavity. Do not use the lemon skin, as it will result in a bitter flavor. Add 1 sprig of thyme, rosemary and parsley to the cavity. With the remaining sprigs, pull the chicken skin away from the breast meat. Place the sprigs between the skin and meat. Place the truffle oil in the cavity as well. Truss the chicken legs together with butcher's twine. Sew the bird's opening shut with a large poultry needle. Fold the wings back behind the bird. Generously rub them with butter.

For the cooking process: Place a roasting rack in a sheet pan. Place the chicken on the rack breast-side up. Place it in a 500 degree oven for 10 minutes. Lower the heat to 325 to bake for about 1 hour. Baste and turn the chicken every 15 minutes. When a thermometer placed deep into the chicken's thigh reads 165, the chicken is ready.

For the plate: This chicken is best served in pieces, not sliced. Separate all pieces onto a large serving tray.

Recommended wines:
Fetzer Barre Select Pinot Noir 2000 (Mendocino County, California, USA)
Chateau De Chassagne Montrachet Blanc "En Pimont" 2000 (Burgundy, France)

Braised Confit of Duck with Monkfish

Braised duck:
6 duck legs, cooked as described below and meat pulled
1 cup demi-glaze
1 fresh thyme sprig
1 cup orange juice
salt and pepper to taste
2 tablespoons unsalted butter
1 cup red wine
½ cup Filippo Berio olive oil

Monkfish:
6 ounces monkfish per serving, tied and rolled
½ cup white wine
salt and pepper to taste
1 teaspoon white truffle paste
assorted vegetables cut into half-inch-thick strips
2 tablespoons Filippo Berio olive oil

For the duck: Fill a skillet three-fourths with oil. Simmer the duck legs in the skillet for about 1½ hours. Remove the skillet from the heat, but let the duck stand in the oil for 2½ hours. Remove it from the pan, but discard the oil. While the duck is still warm, pull the meat off the bone. In a separate saucepan, add the demi-glaze. Bring the mixture to a low simmer. Add the fresh thyme, orange juice, wine and butter. Reduce by one-third. The sauce should be a thick syrup texture. Add the duck. Coat well.

For the monkfish: Add the oil to a sauté pan. Sear the monkfish on all sides. Empty the oil from the pan. Put the monkfish in the oven for 12 to 15 minutes on 425 degrees. When the fish is done, set it aside. Add the wine and truffle paste to the pan. Let it reduce. For the vegetables, sauté with olive oil until firm but crisp. Season with salt and pepper.

For the plate: Artistically arrange the vegetables in a large plate's center. Place the monkfish on the bed of vegetables. Place a tablespoon of shredded duck confit on top of the monkfish. Spoon some sauce from the duck around the fish.

Recommended wines:
Montevina Zinfandel Amador 2000 Red (Amador County, California, USA)
Taz Pinot Gris 2002 White (Santa Barbara County, Santa Monica Valley, California, USA)

Duck Breast á l'Orange with a Twist

3 whole duck breasts, preferably Long Island duckling
1 16-ounce bottle orange soda
2 cups orange juice
½ cup lime juice · ½ cup lemon juice
¼ cup orange-flavored brandy · ¼ cup orange marmalade
2 tablespoons canola oil
¼ cup Italian parsley, chopped · ¼ cup tarragon, chopped

For the marinade: Mix all the ingredients — except the duck — in a large mixing bowl. Stir so that all the ingredients are well mixed.

For the duck: Place the duck breasts skin-side down on a cutting board. Using a sharp knife, make a cut down the breast's center to separate the two lobes. Turn the breasts over, with the skin-side up. With the knife, make several diagonal cuts across the breast's skin, cutting through the skin to the meat but not through the meat. Turn the breast to repeat the cuts in the opposite direction to achieve a diamond pattern. Place the breasts in the marinade. Let them sit for 3 to 4 hours (or overnight) — covered and in the refrigerator. Heat a large cast-iron pan on the stovetop. Remove the duck from the marinade. Shake off any excess. Salt and pepper both sides of the breast. Place the breasts in the hot pan, skin-side down. Do not add any fat or oil to the pan, as the skin has more than enough to keep the breast from sticking. Brown both sides of the breast well, but do not burn. Remove the breasts from the pan. Place them in a shallow roasting pan.

For the sauce: Strain the marinade to remove all the herbs. Pour it into a heavy saucepan. Reduce the mixture by half. Pour the sauce over the duck. Place the duck in a preheated oven at 375 degrees for 10 minutes or until the duck is medium rare.

For the plate: Slice the duck on an angle. Place 1 breast on each plate. Spread the breast to form a fan pattern. Spoon the sauce over the meat before serving. Garnish with a fresh tarragon sprig.

Serves 6.

Recommended drinks:
Kunde Viognier 1999 (Sanoma, California, USA)
Tuaca Orange Liquor:
Chill a rim glass with orange sugar. Strain it into a martini glass.

Braised Chicken with Tomatoes and Thyme

1 large whole chicken, about 3 to 5 pounds
1 cup dry white wine
¼ cup white vinegar
1 fresh thyme sprig
2 garlic cloves
¼ pound unsalted butter
4 teaspoons Filippo Berio olive oil
1 20-ounce can whole tomatoes, seeded and diced
1 cilantro sprig
3 ounces piquillo peppers
2 shallots, peeled and sliced
salt and fresh ground pepper

For the chicken: Wash the chicken in salted water. Dry it well. Cut the bird into 8 pieces. Cut the breasts in half.

For the cooking: Heat the oil and the butter in a large skillet to brown the chicken, garlic and shallots. Roughly chop the thyme before adding it to the skillet. Turn the chicken to crisp the skin on both sides. Pour in the white wine. Raise the heat to reduce the wine. Add the peeled and seeded tomatoes, seasoning them with just the black pepper for now. Add the piquillo peppers. Reduce the heat. Cover the skillet with a lid for about 30 minutes. Add salt to taste.

For the dish: This classic dish goes great with white rice but would also go well with roasted potatoes.

Recommended wines:
Bolla Amarone Del Vallpolicella 1996 (Veneto, Italy)
Cantina Di Montalcino Chianti Classico Reserva 2000 (Tuscan, Italy)

Chicken Burritos

1 small onion, chopped
2 garlic cloves, minced
1 tablespoon canola oil
1 pound boneless skinless chicken breasts, cut into 2-inch strips
1 teaspoon cumin
12 ounces black beans, cooked
1½ cups tomato salsa
1 teaspoon chili powder
6 flour tortillas
1 cup Monterey Jack cheese, shredded
6 cups fresh romaine lettuce, chopped
½ cup sour cream

For the filling: In a large sauté pan, heat the oil over medium heat. When hot, add the onion and garlic. Sauté until tender. Add the chicken. Brown it well. Cook until no pink remains in the chicken. Stir in the beans, cumin, chili powder and the half-cup of salsa. Cook uncovered on medium-low heat until the mixture starts to thicken. Keep warm. In a separate, large sauté pan, heat the tortillas one at a time until soft. Place them in a large plastic container with a lid until the filling is done.

To fold the burritos: Place the tortillas on a flat surface. Place a half-cup of filling on each tortilla. Sprinkle shredded cheese on each. To fold the tortilla: Take the end closest to you, fold it over the filling, pull the end back toward you to tightly encase the filling, fold the sides in and then roll tightly.

For the plate: Serve the burritos with the shredded lettuce, sour cream, salsa and shredded Monterey Jack. Serve the burritos while still hot.

Serves 6.

Braised Chicken Breasts in Sun-Dried Tomato Sauce

4 chicken breasts, skin and bone on
2 tablespoons Filippo Berio olive oil
6 large garlic cloves, thinly sliced
1 cup dry white wine
1 cup heavy cream
½ cup sun-dried tomatoes, thinly sliced
¼ cup basil, thinly sliced
1 tablespoon fresh oregano
salt and pepper to taste

For the chicken: Season the chicken with salt and pepper on both sides. In a heavy cast-iron pan, heat the olive oil on medium. Add the chicken. Brown it well on both sides. Add the garlic. Sauté for 1 minute. Remove the chicken from the pan, but keep the pieces warm.

For the sauce: Deglaze the pan with the white wine. Add the tomatoes. Mix well. Add the heavy cream. Bring the sauce to a simmer. Add the chicken back to the sauce. Cover the pan. Cook on a low heat. Simmer until the chicken is cooked. Add half the basil and the oregano to the pan. Mix well. Quickly bring the sauce to a boil to thicken it. Remove the chicken. Place the pieces on plates. Remove the sauce from the heat, add the remaining basil to the pan and then toss. Adjust the seasoning with salt and pepper. Spoon the sauce over the chicken.

Serves 4.

Chicken Cacciatore or Hunter's Style

1 large chicken, 5 to 6 pounds and cut into 6 pieces
all-purpose flour, as needed
6 tablespoons Filippo Berio olive oil
1 pound mushrooms, sliced
1 medium onion, chopped
1 red bell pepper, diced
5 garlic cloves, sliced
1 teaspoon fresh oregano, chopped
1 cup fresh marinara sauce
1 pound fresh plum tomatoes, seeded, cored and diced
1 cup chicken stock
1 cup red wine
3 tablespoons capers
1 anchovy fillet
½ cup fresh basil, chopped

For the chicken: Season the flour with salt and pepper. Place the flour in a large plastic bag. Add the chicken. Shake well to coat the chicken. Shake excess flour off. Discard the plastic bag. In a large, heavy skillet, heat half the olive oil on medium heat. Add the chicken. Brown the pieces well on all sides. Remove the chicken from the pan. Pour off the excess fat. Heat the remaining olive oil in the pan. Add the mushrooms, onion, pepper, garlic, oregano and anchovy fillet to the pan. Cook until the onions are tender. Mix in the marinara, plum tomatoes, stock and wine. Add the chicken back to the pan. Add the capers. Bring to a boil. Cover the pan. Reduce to low. Simmer until the chicken is tender.

For the table: Remove the chicken from the pan. Place the pieces on a large platter. Return the sauce to the stovetop. Bring it to a boil. Allow the sauce to thicken. Add the basil before removing the sauce from the heat. Spoon any excess fat off the top of the sauce. Pour the sauce over the chicken. Serve family-style.

Serves 4 to 6.

Braised Quail with Bolla Amarone

8 quails, cleaned
8 large bacon strips
¼ pound morel mushrooms
1½ cups foie gras, Grade B and cleaned
2 tablespoons tomato paste
2 cups chicken stock
5 slices 1-inch thick challah bread, cut into half-inch squares
3 cups Bolla Amarone red wine
2 onions, chopped
2 carrots, peeled and diced
2 celery stalks, diced
½ cup Filippo Berio olive oil
4 ounces white navy beans, cooked
salt and pepper to taste

For the quails: Lay the quails on a clean work surface. Season them with salt and pepper. Be sure to season inside the cavities as well. Wrap 1 strip of bacon around each quail's chest.

For the braising: Place a casserole dish on the stovetop on medium heat. Add the oil. Sear each quail on all sides until golden brown. Remove the quail from the casserole dish. Add the carrots, morels, onions and celery. Sauté the vegetables until lightly brown. Place the quail back-side down neatly in the pan next to each other. Spread the beans throughout the dish. Place the casserole dish back on the heat. Deglaze with the wine. Add the chicken stock, challah bread and tomato paste. Allow the mixture to reduce slightly over high heat. Add the foie gras on top of the bread. Remove the casserole dish from the heat. Place it in a 375 degree oven for 45 minutes. Every 10 minutes, open the oven to baste the birds with the jus. Skim any excess fat from the pan. Adjust for seasoning with salt and pepper.

Chef's note: This dish is very rich. Even though I have the beans as a starch, I still love to serve this dish with white rice. Don't forget to shave some Parmigiano-Reggiano cheese on top.

Serves 4.

Recommended drink:
Bolla Amarone 1998 (Veneto, Italy)

Meat ar

d Game

Fillets of Venison au Poive

4 6-ounce venison loin fillets
1 teaspoon salt
1 teaspoon pepper
4 ounces unsalted butter
2 ounces Filippo Berio olive oil
2 ounces brandy
½ cup red wine
½ cup beef stock
1 ounce green peppercorns in brine

For the venison: Melt half the butter in a hot sauté pan. Add olive oil to the melted butter. Season the venison with salt and pepper on both sides. Place the venison in the pan, sear quickly on both sides and then remove it from the pan.

For the sauce: Remove the pan from the heat. Add the brandy to deglaze the pan. Place the pan back on a moderate heat, but be very careful, as the brandy will flame. When the flame subsides, add the red wine and stock. Reduce by half. Add the green peppercorns. Continue to cook on a low heat for 5 minutes. Place the venison back in the pan. Cook for another 5 minutes. Adjust the seasoning with salt and black pepper. Remove the venison from the pan. Add the remaining butter to the sauce to thicken it.

For the plate: Place the venison on a plate. Spoon some sauce over the fillets.

Recommended wines:
Chateau De Beaucastel Chatauneuf-Du-Pape 1999 (Rhone Valley, France)
Bonterra Viognier 2002 (Mendocino, California, USA)

Braised Short Ribs with Truffle Polenta

10 pounds beef short ribs, back straps off and split
all-purpose flour, as needed
1 onion, chopped
1 carrot, chopped
3 celery stalks, chopped
2 quarts red wine
2 quarts demi-glaze
8 ounces Filippo Berio olive oil
½-pound butter
1 pound cornmeal
4 quarts chicken stock
4 ounces crème fraiche
4 tablespoons truffle oil
salt and pepper to taste

For the ribs: Heat the olive oil in a large pot on the stovetop. Season the flour with salt and pepper. Dredge the ribs in flour. Sear them in the hot oil. Add the chopped vegetables. Sweat them until the onions are translucent. Deglaze with the red wine. Bring to a boil. Reduce by half. Add the demi-glaze. Bring the mixture back to a boil. Lower to a simmer. Cook the ribs for about 4 hours or until they're fork-tender. Pull the ribs from the pot, but keep them warm. Strain the liquid through a fine mesh. Bring the liquid back to a boil, season with salt and pepper and then reserve it for the dish.

For the polenta: In heavy-bottom saucepan, melt the butter. Add the cornmeal. In stages, add the chicken stock. As the liquid absorbs, add more stock — while constantly stirring — until the polenta is smooth and the grittiness is gone. Stir in the truffle oil and crème fraiche.

For the dish: Spoon a generous helping of polenta onto the dish's middle. Take a rib, perch it on top of the polenta and then ladle the reserved demi-glaze onto the meat. This dish is great for cool autumn evenings. For leftover short ribs, consider the following uses: Pull the meat off the bones to make a stuffing for ravioli or toss the meat into a pasta dish with a hearty red sauce.

Recommended drink:
Castello Banfi Brunello di Montalcino 1999 (Tuscany, Italy)

Polenta-Crusted Rabbit with Wild Mushrooms

2 fryer rabbits, cut into 8 pieces
3 cups polenta or fine cornmeal
½ cup canola oil
salt and pepper to taste
¼ cup unsalted butter
1 cup brown or beef stock
2 thyme sprigs
¼ cup wine
2 shallots, finely minced
1½-pounds mixed wild mushrooms, such as chanterelles, oyster or porcini (use more than one type)
½ cup heavy cream

For the rabbit: Cut the rabbit into pieces or have your butcher do it for you. Season the rabbit with salt and pepper. Pour polenta into a shallow dish. Season with salt and pepper. Dredge the rabbit on both sides in the polenta. Place it aside. Clean the mushrooms well to remove any soil. Cut them into quarters. Place them aside. Mince the shallots. Place them aside.

For the stew: In a heavy skillet, heat the oil. Add the rabbit, browning well on both sides. Do not burn. Remove the rabbit to a dish, but keep it warm. Pour out most of the remaining oil before adding butter. Return the pan to the heat. Add shallots. Sauté them until limp. Add the mushrooms. Toss them in the pan. Deglaze with the red wine. Add the thyme. Season with salt and pepper. Add the stock and cream. Allow the mixture to slightly reduce. Return the rabbit to the pan. Place the rabbit on top of the mushrooms. Do not stir. Reduce the heat. Cook for 15 to 20 minutes.

For the plate: Remove the rabbit from the pan. Place it in a serving dish. Spoon the mushrooms over the rabbit, but reserve some liquid in the pan. Return the pan back to the heat. Reduce the liquid by half. To serve, place the rabbit and mushrooms on individual plates. Spoon the sauce over each serving. Serve with braised red cabbage.

Serves 4 to 6.

Recommended wines:
Chateau Grand Cassagne 2003 Rose (Western Rhone, France)
Acacia Pinot Carneros Noir 2002 Red (Carneros, California, USA)
Krug Rosé NV (nonvintage)
Sparkling (Champagne, France)

Braised Pork Roulade

1 piece boneless pork shoulder, excess fat removed, rolled and tied
3 cups red wine
3 cups beef stock
3 tablespoons Filippo Berio olive oil
salt and pepper as needed
1 celery rib, chopped
1 garlic clove, minced
½ cup zucchini, skin only and minced
½ cup yellow squash, skin only and minced
½ cup red onion, minced
½ cup carrots, minced
4 plum tomatoes, peeled and chopped
1 tablespoon tomato paste
2 tablespoon shallots, diced

For the pork: Season the pork well with salt and pepper. Heat the olive oil in a Dutch oven until it's smoking. Brown the pork on all sides. Add the onion, celery and carrots. Cook until just starting to brown. Add the garlic, brown it, deglaze with the red wine and then add the beef stock. Add the tomatoes and tomato paste. Cover the pot before placing it in a 350 degree oven for 1½ hours or until the pork is very tender. Remove the pork from the pot. Strain the sauce, being sure to press the vegetables to get all the flavor. Place the sauce in a saucepan. Reduce it until it's thickened. Slice the pork after removing the string, but keep it warm until ready to serve.

For the vegetables: In a sauté pan, heat the butter. Add the zucchini and squash. Cook until tender. Season with salt and pepper.

For the plate: Place the sautéed squashes in a platter's center. Circle them with the sliced pork. Spoon the sauce onto only the meat. Serve family-style.

Recommended wines:
Newton Cabernet Sauvignon 2000 Red Unfiltered (Sonoma, California, USA)
Simi Cabernet Sauvignon 2001 Red (Sonoma, California, USA)

Duo of Beef

2 cups dry red wine
⅓ cup shallots, chopped fine
1 small carrot, chopped fine
2 thyme sprigs
1 tablespoon butter
2 cups veal demi-glaze
¼ teaspoon salt
4 6-ounce beef tenderloin fillets
cracked black pepper to taste
1 tablespoon Filippo Berio olive oil
1 pound prosciutto di Parma, thinly sliced
butcher's twine

For the sauce: In a saucepan, add the red wine, shallot, carrot and thyme. Bring to a boil. Reduce until approximately a half-cup is left. Add the demi-glaze. Return the mixture to a boil. Remove it from the heat. Strain it twice, being sure to press the solids to remove as much flavor as possible. Pour the sauce into a sauté pan. Bring it to a boil again. Add the butter. Reduce the heat to a simmer, being sure to whisk the sauce well. Adjust the seasoning. Keep warm until the beef is ready.

For the beef: Clean and trim all fat and silver skin from the tenderloin. Season to taste with the cracked pepper. Wrap the prosciutto around the beef, being sure to cover all sides. Using the butcher's twine, tie the prosciutto securely in place. Heat a sauté pan on high heat. Add the oil. Sear the beef evenly on all sides. Lower the heat. Cook the beef until it reaches a desired temperature — 130 degrees for medium rare.

For the plate: The beef would go well with risotto or potatoes. Place the beef in a plate's center. Pool the sauce around it. Garnish with the fresh thyme sprig.

Chef's note: When cooking with wine, NEVER use that seasoned stuff from the supermarket shelves. A good rule of thumb: If you can't drink it, don't cook with it.

Recommended wines:
Franciscan Oakville Estates Cabernet 2001 Red (Napa Valley, California, USA)
Kendall Jackson Grand Reserve Cabernet 1999 Red (Sonoma, California, USA)

Pan-Smoked and Cinnamon-Crusted Rack of Lamb

2 racks of lamb, bones frenched
2 teaspoons ground cinnamon
1 teaspoon kosher salt · 1 teaspoon coarsely ground black pepper
¼ cup Filippo Berio olive oil
1 cup wood chips (hickory or apple wood are best)
2 shallots, finely minced
1 cup red wine · 1 cup demi-glaze or brown stock
1 thyme sprig · 4 mint leaves, cut into strips
1 teaspoon butter · salt and pepper to taste

Special equipment needed: Stovetop smoker*

For the smoker: Soak the wood chips in water for 1 hour. Place them in the stovetop smoker. Heat it on low. When smoke starts to come from the sides, the smoker is ready for the meat. *If you do not have a stovetop smoker, take a heavy roasting pan, place the chips on the roaster's bottom, place a wire rack over the chips and then cover the roaster with aluminum foil.

For the lamb: Mix the cinnamon, kosher salt and coarse pepper together. Rub the racks of lamb with this mixture on all sides. In a sauté pan, heat the olive oil. Place the lamb meat-side down in the oil. Sear the lamb well on both sides. Remove the lamb from the pan, but reserve some oil in the pan for the sauce. Open the smoker. Be careful when opening the smoker to avoid inhaling the smoke. Place the lamb on a rack in the smoker. Close the smoker. Turn the heat up to medium. Smoke the lamb for 10 minutes for rare and 12 to 15 minutes for medium. The longer the lamb stays in the smoker, the more smoked flavor it will have.

For the sauce: In the sauté pan with the reserved oil, sauté the shallots until limp. Deglaze with the red wine. Reduce by half. Add the thyme, demi-glaze and mint leaves. Finish the sauce with the butter. Adjust the seasoning with salt and pepper.

For the plate: Cut the lamb into chops by slicing between the bones. Artistically arrange them on a plate. Spoon the sauce around the lamb. Serve 3 chops per person. As a suggestion, serve with couscous or risotto.

Serves 4.

Recommended wine:
Travaglini Gattinara 1999 Red (Piedmont, Italy)

Carnaroli Risotto with Braised Pork and White Truffles

Pork:
1 pound pork shoulder, boned, fat removed, rolled and tied
2 quarts red wine
4 tablespoons tomato paste
1 shallot, peeled and diced
1 bay leaf
salt and pepper to taste
½ cup Filippo Berio olive oil

Risotto:
2 teaspoons butter
1½ teaspoons lard
½ shallot bulb, peeled and diced
1 cup white wine
2 cups Carnaroli risotto
5 cups chicken stock
2 ounces Pecorino Romano cheese, grated
1 ounce white truffle oil
salt and pepper to taste

For the pork: In a skillet on medium heat, add the olive oil. Cook the oil until it's smoking hot. Place the pork roll in the pan, browning evenly on all sides. Take the pork from the skillet, but discard the oil. Return the pot back to the stove — along with the pork — and deglaze with red wine. Add the shallot, bay leaf and the tomato paste. Braise on simmer for about 1 hour and 45 minutes, checking the meat's tenderness every 15 minutes. When the pork is done, take the string off. Keep warm until ready to serve.

For the risotto: Melt the butter and the lard in a large pot. Add the diced shallot. Cook until translucent. Add the wine. Bring the mixture to a boil. Lower the heat to stir in the rice, constantly turning the rice to avoid sticking to the pan's bottom. Add the stock 1 cup at a time, adding more when the rice has absorbed the liquid. When the rice has released its starch and is al dente, remove it from the heat. Add the cheese, truffle oil and the salt to taste.

For the plate: Cut the pork into thick slices. Place the risotto on a large platter, arranging the pork around it. Garnish with fresh parsley and basil.

Chef's note: Don't be afraid to use lard. It actually has less saturated fat than butter and adds a tremendous amount of flavor.

Lamb Carpaccio with Tuscan Beans

2 pounds lean, boneless lamb loin
3 heirloom tomatoes, such as Brandywine, Green Zebra, Purple Cherokee (use different varieties for a more colorful dish)
1 bunch basil
2 fresh oregano sprigs
¼ cup Italian parsley, chopped
6 tablespoons Filippo Berio olive oil
¼ cup good-quality balsamic vinegar
salt and pepper to taste
10 ounces dry white kidney beans
2 bay leaves
1 small rosemary branch
1 small red onion, finely chopped
6 ounces Parmigiano-Reggiano cheese

For the lamb: Cut small slices of lamb — about 2 to 3 ounces each. Place between 2 sheets of parchment paper or plastic wrap. Pound the lamb as thin as possible with a meat mallet or a heavy cast-iron pan. Wrap the lamb. Refrigerate until ready to use.

For the beans: Wash the beans thoroughly. Pick through them to remove any dirt or stones. Place the beans in a large bowl. Cover them with cold water. Let the beans sit overnight. When the beans are ready, place them in a large pot covered with water. Add the bay leaves, rosemary, salt and pepper to taste and then bring it to a boil. Reduce the heat. Cook uncovered until beans are tender. Drain and cool. When cool, add the chopped onion and 3 tablespoons of olive oil. Adjust the seasoning. Mix well.

For the plate: Arrange the lamb on a large serving platter. Slice the tomatoes. Arrange them on top of the lamb. Slice the basil thinly. Peel the oregano leaves from the stems. Spread the leaves and the parsley on top of the tomatoes. Mix the remaining olive oil and the balsamic vinegar together. Season with salt and pepper. Pour the mixture over the tomatoes and lamb. In the platter's middle, arrange the beans. Place shavings of Parmigiano-Reggiano cheese on the platter before serving.

Serves 4 to 6.

Recommended wines:
Edmeads Zinfandel 2000 Red (Mendocino County, California, USA)
McPherson Shiraz Red (Eastern Australia)

OLD BAY
Taste This!
TasteThis!

Dijon-Mustard-Crusted Rack of Lamb

2 half-racks of Colorado spring lamb (or another spring lamb, such as New Zealand)
4 tablespoons Dijon mustard
4 ounces seasoned Japanese breadcrumbs (Panko)
3 ounces Filippo Berio olive oil
1 fresh sage sprig, minced
kosher salt and cracked black pepper to taste

For the lamb: Rub the lamb with a clean rag to absorb any excess liquid. The lamb will sear best if it's as dry as possible. On a clean work surface, season the lamb with salt and pepper on both sides.

For searing the lamb: In a large sauté pan, heat the oil on high. When the oil is very hot, add the lamb, meat-side down. Leave the lamb down on that side for a good 5 minutes. The object is to get the lamb good and crispy. Take the lamb from the pan. Place it in a 375 degree oven for 10 minutes, seared-side up. This will bring the lamb to a temperature of medium rare. Remove it from the oven. Set it aside.

For the final stage: Spread the Dijon mustard over the side that was seared. Pack the seasoned breadcrumbs and fresh sage on top of the mustard, creating a firm crust. Place the lamb back in the oven, crust-side up. When the breadcrumbs are golden brown, remove the lamb from the oven. The lamb will be medium rare. Slice the racks between each bone to create chops.

Chef's note: When you go to your local butcher and ask for a baby rack of lamb, chances are it's all cleaned and ready to go. However, in the event that it's not, ask for the lamb to be frenched with the chine bone out. This will explain to the butcher that you would like the lamb oven-ready. I prefer to serve lamb rare to medium rare, especially young spring lamb. If you prefer your meat well done, allow the lamb to cook longer before crusting it with the breadcrumbs.

Serves 4.

Recommended wine:
Babich Syrah Hawkes Bay Red (Auckland, New Zealand)

Woodsman's Feast

6 large pheasants, cut in half
1 pound fresh morel mushrooms (substitute dry if fresh are unavailable)
1 pound wood nail mushrooms, available in Asian markets
3 cups veal demi-glaze
1 tablespoon sliced shallots
12 baby orange carrots, poached (see method below)
12 baby yellow carrots, poached (see method below)
1 tablespoon unsalted butter
1 pound baby Brussels sprouts
2 cups red wine (Amarone preferred)
1 large spaghetti squash
1 cup polenta or fine cornmeal
2½ cups whole milk
1 teaspoon fresh tarragon, minced
kosher salt to taste
fresh ground black pepper
½ pound Parmigiano-Reggiano cheese, grated
¼ cup crème fraiche (if not available, use sour cream)
2 slices cocktail-size pumpernickel, toasted
1 tablespoon Filippo Berio olive oil
1 tablespoon salted butter

For the spaghetti squash (which should be done 4 hours in advance): Cut the squash in half lengthwise. Roast it facedown in a pan for 45 minutes at 350 degrees. To prevent the squash from sticking and browning, add 2 cups of water to the pan's bottom. This will also help the squash cook quicker by steaming it. Put the squash in the refrigerator for 2 hours to cool. Fork out the filling. It will come apart in strands. Set aside until ready to assemble.

For the pheasant: Cut the pheasant in half so that you will have a wing and a breast attached to each half. Season with a pinch of salt and pepper. In a heavy cast-iron pan, add a small amount of oil on medium heat. When the oil smokes, add the pheasant, skin-side down. Add the shallots. When both are golden brown, remove them from the heat. Deglaze with the red wine. Return the pan to the heat, continuing to cook. Add the veal demi-glaze and the morel mushrooms. Continue to simmer on low heat — covered halfway with a lid — for 20 minutes.

For the vegetables: Bring 1 gallon of salted water to a boil. When the water reaches a boil, shut the heat off. Add the peeled carrots and Brussels sprouts to the water. After 2½ minutes, strain the vegetables. Let them sit in an ice bath for 15 minutes. Strain again. Transfer them to a kitchen towel to let them dry until ready to plate.

For the polenta: In a one-quart saucepan, bring the milk to a boil. Add a pinch of salt and pepper to taste. Add the cornmeal into the boiling milk, stirring slowly with a whisk. Lower the heat. Continue to whisk constantly to prevent lumping. When the cornmeal is smooth, remove it from the heat. Stir in the crème fraiche, grated cheese and tarragon.

For the plate (the composition is done in three separate steps):
First: Two tablespoons of cooked polenta should be put down first. Place 1 pheasant half over the polenta. Spoon the wild mushroom sauce over the pheasant.
Second: In a small saucepan, add 1 tablespoon of salted butter with the squash to reheat. Place the cocktail toast in the plate's center, with the hot squash on top of the toast.
Third: In a small saucepan, add the wood nail mushrooms to 1 tablespoon of butter. When the mushrooms have cooked slightly, add the poached vegetables. When the vegetables and mushrooms are tender and soft, remove them from the heat. Adjust the seasoning with salt and pepper. Artistically arrange the vegetables and mushrooms on the plate.

Makes 12 portions.

Surf and Turf — My Way

2 pounds Russet potatoes · 1 pound Idaho potatoes
2 tablespoons bread flour, sifted · 1 tablespoon cake flour, sifted
3 tablespoons crème fraiche
2 large, brown organic eggs · 2 egg yolks
salt and pepper to taste
5 6-ounce lobster tails, removed from the shell
2 pounds unsalted butter
5 quail eggs
1 teaspoon unsalted butter
1 large Idaho potato, roasted
½ pound salted butter
1 teaspoon truffle oil
1 teaspoon chives, minced
5 strips bacon, cooked well
2 pounds beef short ribs, boneless and cleaned
8 cups red wine, Bonterra Cabernet Sauvignon preferred
2 cups veal demi-glaze
5 sea scallops, U-10 size and side muscle removed
3 teaspoons Filippo Berio olive oil
kosher salt to taste · black pepper to taste

For the blini: Clean the Russet potatoes before baking them in a 350 degree oven until fully cooked. Cut the cooked potato in half to scrape the insides into a bowl. Press the potatoes through a China cap, discarding the skin. In a stand mixer on slow speed with a paddle, add the bread flour into the potatoes. Add the crème fraiche while stirring quickly. Add the cake flour while continuing to mix thoroughly. Slowly add the egg yolks one at a time, continuing to mix. Add the whole eggs. The mixture should be thin. Put the mixture in a squeeze bottle.

For cooking the blini: In a nonstick pan on medium heat, melt 1 teaspoon of butter. Lower the heat to low. Squeeze half-dollar circles of batter into the lightly buttered pan. Brown on both sides for at least 1 minute. The blini will rise — a sign of being fully cooked. This recipe makes 15 blinis.

For the braised short ribs: Clean the boneless short ribs of any fat and cartilage. In a medium-sized pot, add 2 teaspoons of olive oil. Brown the meat on all sides. Deglaze with red wine. Add the veal demi-glaze. Lower to a simmer. Cook for 2½ hours until very tender. The meat should be glazed from the reduction of wine and veal demi-glaze. When the ribs are done, remove them from the pan, but keep them warm until ready to plate.

For the lobster tail confit: In a medium saucepan, add 2 pounds of unsalted butter. Melt it slowly. Slice the lobster meat in half lengthwise. Add the lobster tails to the butter. Cook for 15 minutes at a constant temperature of 145 degrees. Take the lobster from the butter. Reserve it until ready to plate. When plating, return the lobster to the hot butter for a quick reheat.

For the sea scallops: In a nonstick pan on high heat, add the teaspoon of olive oil. When the oil is hot, add the cleaned scallops to the pan. Cook for 3 minutes on each side.

For the truffle mashed potatoes: Peel the hot, roasted Idaho potatoes. Put them in a stand mixer on low speed with a paddle. Add the teaspoon of truffle oil and the half-pound of butter. Continue to mix until smooth. Add chives, salt and pepper to taste. Keep warm until ready to plate.

For the quail eggs: In a nonstick pan, melt 1 teaspoon of unsalted butter on medium heat. Carefully crack the quail egg into the pan. Cook it sunny-side up for 2 minutes — never turning the egg yolk over. Take the egg from the pan with a small spatula. Set it aside until serving.

For the plate (composition is done in two steps):
First: Add 3 cooked blinis to one side of the plate. Stack the braised glazed short ribs on top of the blini. Place the lobster confit on top of the short ribs.
Second: Place a tablespoon of white truffle mashed potatoes opposite the blinis. Add the seared scallop. Place the quail egg on top of the scallops. Finally, place the cooked bacon strip in the center.

Serves 5.

Recommended drink:

Formula #21 Punch:

1 bottle Finlandia vodka
1 bottle Retor Chardonnay
2 quarts pineapple juice
½ cup lime juice
2 quarts chilled club soda
sugar to taste

Mix the ingredients in a punch bowl.

Grilled Sirloin with Mole Demi-Glaze

1 ounce chipotle pepper
1 jalapeño pepper, seeds removed and diced
1 onion, diced
4 ounces Filippo Berio olive oil
2 ounces garlic cloves, peeled and diced
8 ounces almonds, sliced and blanched
2 ounces chili powder
1 teaspoon anise seeds
1 tablespoon fresh ginger, grated
1 teaspoon ground cinnamon
1 tablespoon fresh thyme leaves, pulled from the stems
1 pint demi-glaze
4 tablespoons peanut butter
4 ounces dark chocolate
2 ounces toasted sesame seeds
3 ounces butter
4 12-ounce prime sirloin steaks

For the mole demi-glaze: In a saucepan, add the olive oil to brown the onions, garlic and jalapeño. Add the anise, chili powder, chipotle and cinnamon. Deglaze with the demi-glaze. Whisk in the peanut butter. Strain through a fine-mesh strainer. Gently stir in the chocolate and butter. Keep warm until the steaks are ready.

For the steaks: Season the steaks with sea salt and black pepper. Grill to medium rare. Let them rest for 5 minutes.

For the dish: Place 1 steak on the plate. Ladle 4 ounces of demi-glaze on the steak.

For the garnish: When cooking with ingredients that you normally don't see together — such as chocolate and beef — you want your guests to realize what they're eating. I suggest garnishing the plate in this fashion: You could use a little shaved chocolate or a dusting of cocoa powder, but for this plate, I prefer to use a sliver from a chocolate candy bar. Taste this!

Recommended wines:
Moriah Zinfandel 1999 (Mendocino, California, USA)
Petite Syrah Eagle Point Edmeades Estates 1998 (Mendocino, California, USA)

FRENCH
OAK AGED
Marinella
DELL'AMORE
PREMIUM
MARINARA
SAUCE
Pareve
PUTTANESCA

EDEN

Texas-Style Barbeque Brisket

1 piece whole beef brisket, approximately 12 to 15 pounds
1 cup brown sugar
½ cup kosher salt
2 tablespoons chili powder
1 teaspoon cumin
1 tablespoon coarsely ground pepper
1 quart thin tomato sauce
1 12-ounce bottle dark beer
1 cup molasses
1 cup dark corn syrup
1 cup honey
½ cup malt vinegar
hickory wood chips, as needed

For the brisket: Trim some fat from the brisket. It should have about a quarter-inch of fat all around. Mix the brown sugar, kosher salt, chili powder, cumin and black pepper together. Mix well. Rub the mixture onto the brisket, covering both sides. Wrap it tightly in plastic wrap to refrigerate overnight.

For the sauce: Add the remaining ingredients — except for the wood chips — to a saucepan. Bring the mixture to a boil. Reduce to a medium heat. Stir occasionally to prevent sticking. Let the sauce reduce by one-fourth. Remove it from heat.

For the grill: Remove the brisket from the plastic. Place it in a shallow aluminum pan large enough to hold it. Add enough water to cover the pan's bottom. Put wood chips in a smoker box. Place it on a hot gas grill with a full tank of gas. When the chips start to smoke, place the pan in the grill's center. Reduce the heat to low. Add more wood chips as needed to keep a good flow of smoke. Check the water level; add as needed. The brisket needs long, slow-cooking and will take 6 to 8 hours, depending on size. It's done when shreds of meat can be easily pulled off.

For the plate: Trim the remaining fat off. Remove the deckle, which is the small, fattier piece of meat on top. With a sharp slicing knife, cut the meat against the grain into thin slices. Place them on a plate. Pour the sauce over the meat. Serve with coleslaw.

Serves 10 to 12.

Recommended drink:
3 ounces Woodford Reserve single-batch bourbon over ice (Kentucky, USA)

Grilled Pork Tenderloin with Mango Peach Salsa

2 large fresh pork tenderloins (about 3 to 5 pounds)
1 teaspoon cumin
1 teaspoon dark chili powder
½ teaspoon ground coriander
½ teaspoon kosher salt
1 teaspoon coarsely ground pepper
3 large ripe mangoes, peeled and diced small
3 ripe yellow peaches, skin on and diced small
1 small red onion, finely diced
½ teaspoon cilantro, finely chopped
2 fresh chile peppers, seeds removed and finely diced
¼ cup fresh lime juice
¼ cup fresh lemon juice
¼ cup Filippo Berio olive oil

For the tenderloin: Mix the cumin, chili powder, coriander, salt and pepper together. Rub the mixture on the tenderloins, coating them well. Refrigerate for 2 to 3 hours. On a hot coal or gas grill, cook them until medium — approximately 150 degrees. Remove the tenderloins from the grill. Serve them with the salsa.

For the salsa: Mix all remaining ingredients well to incorporate the flavors. Refrigerate until ready to use.

For the plate: Cut thin slices of tenderloin. Fan them creatively on a platter. Spoon the salsa over the meat. Serve while the meat is still hot.

Serves 5 to 6.

Recommended wines:
Ferrari-Carano Merlot 2000 (Sonoma County, California, USA)
Simi Rose of Cabernet (Sonoma, California, USA)
Domaine Gros Nore Bandol Rose 2003 (Provence, France)

Simply-Elegant Sautéed Pork Liver

8 slices pork liver, cut into paper-thin slices
1 cup flour
½ cup Filippo Berio olive oil
½ cup shallots, sliced
½ bunch fresh chives, diced
juice from 1 lemon
1 tablespoon parsley, chopped
2 bacon strips, chopped
2 tablespoons demi-glaze
salt and white pepper to taste

For the liver: Evenly season the liver with salt and white pepper. Dredge in flour, coating it well but removing any excess flour. In a sauté pan, heat the oil over medium heat. Brown the onions and bacon. Remove them from the pan, leaving any oil in the pan. In the same pan, add the liver. Brown it for 30 seconds on each side. Add the lemon juice and demi-glaze. Cook down slightly. Add chopped parsley and chives. Toss the onion and bacon mixture back in the pan, being sure to evenly coat the onions with the sauce. Remove the pan from the heat. Adjust the seasoning with salt and pepper.

Chef's note: Liver is best served while very hot. Plate immediately — and enjoy. Mother always said to eat your liver because it's good for you!

Serves 4.

Recommended wines:
Michel Picard Cotes du Rhone Red (Rhone Valley, France)
Chateaux Du Campuget Syrah Prestige 2000 Red (Western Rhone, France)

Seared Rib Eye Steaks with Wild Mushroom Merlot Sauce

4 10- to 12-ounce rib eye steaks
2 tablespoons Filippo Berio olive oil
3 tablespoons unsalted butter
6 ounces fresh wild mushrooms, sliced
2 shallots, thinly sliced
1 cup Merlot wine
1 tablespoon fresh rosemary, chopped
kosher salt and coarsely ground pepper to taste

For the steaks: Season both sides of the steaks with salt and pepper. In a heavy cast-iron pan, heat the oil over medium heat until very hot. Add the steaks. Sear them well on both sides. Remove the steaks from the pan, but keep them warm.

For the sauce: Add 1 tablespoon of butter to the pan. Add the shallots. Sauté for 1 minute. Add the mushrooms. Toss them in the pan. Deglaze with the wine. Add the rosemary. Reduce by half. Remove the pan from the heat. Whisk in the remaining butter. Adjust the seasoning. Add the steaks back to the sauce. Cook for 2 minutes. Remove the steaks from the heat. Serve immediately.

Serves 4.

Grandma's Sicilian Meatballs

1 cup fresh breadcrumbs
6 tablespoons milk
⅔ cup Parmigiano-Reggiano cheese, grated
½ cup onion, finely chopped
2 garlic cloves, roasted and smashed
3 tablespoons fresh basil, chopped
2 tablespoons fresh oregano, chopped
2 large eggs
kosher salt and black pepper to taste
1 pound sweet Italian sausage, removed from its casings
1 pound ground round beef
4 tablespoons toasted pine nuts
4 tablespoons raisins

For the meatballs: Mix the breadcrumbs and the milk together. Let the mixture stand for 10 minutes. Mix in all remaining ingredients. Blend well. Using your hands, form 2-inch balls. Grease several baking sheets with oil. Place the balls on sheets. Place them in a preheated 350 degree oven. Cook until the meatballs are brown and cooked through.

Chef's note: Add the meatballs to a freshly made marinara sauce. Serve them with spaghetti for a traditional favorite.

Shepherd's Pie

12 ounces pearl onions
3 medium leeks, whites only and cut into thin strips
2½-pounds boneless lamb shoulder, cut into 1-inch cubes
6 tablespoons all-purpose flour
3½ tablespoons unsalted butter
2 tablespoons garlic, chopped
½ cup dry white wine
1½ teaspoons tomato paste
1 cup fresh beef stock
1 cup water
2 teaspoons fresh thyme leaves, chopped
5 carrots, diced small
2 medium-sized white turnips, peeled and cut into half-inch pieces
kosher salt and black pepper to taste
2½-pounds all-purpose potatoes, peeled and diced large
1 cup heavy cream
½ cup whole milk
6 tablespoons unsalted butter, cold and cut into pieces
salt and white pepper to taste

For the filling: Soak the leeks in cold water to remove any sand. Rinse. Soak again. In a small pot, blanch the onions in boiling water. Transfer them to an ice bath to stop the cooking. Peel and trim the onions. Place the flour in a plastic bag. Season it with salt and pepper. Add the lamb. Shake the bag well to coat the pieces. In a heavy ovenproof casserole dish, melt 2 tablespoons of butter. Add the garlic. Brown it on all sides. Remove the lamb from the dish. Reserve it. Deglaze the dish with the white wine. Scrape any browned pieces from the pan's sides. Add the tomato paste. Blend. Bring the mixture to a boil. Reduce the liquid by half. Add the lamb back into the dish. Add the onions, leeks, carrots, turnips, stock and water. Season with salt and black pepper. Bring the dish to a hard simmer. Remove the dish from the stovetop. Cover it before placing it in a preheated 350 degree oven for 1½ to 2 hours. Stir the mixture several times while cooking.

For the mashed potato topping: Place the diced potatoes in a large pot filled with cold, salted water. Bring it to a boil. Reduce the heat to medium. Cook until the potatoes are tender. Drain, but keep the potatoes hot in the same pot. Before the potatoes are done, bring the cream, milk and butter to a boil in a separate pot. Remove the mixture from the heat. With a potato masher, break up the potatoes. Add the cream mixture. Whip with a hand mixer. Season with salt and white pepper.

To assemble the pie: If the filling has not thickened, melt 1½ tablespoons of butter. Add 2 tablespoons of flour to form a roux. Remove 1 cup of sauce from the baking dish. Add it to the roux. Bring it to a boil. Add it back to the casserole dish. Spoon the potatoes over the lamb evenly and smoothly. Place the pie under a hot broiler. Brown the top well. Serve immediately.

Chef's note: Leftover leg of lamb can be used for the pie or you can substitute ground beef. The potatoes can be piped onto the casserole with a pastry bag and a large star tip for a more dramatic display.

Serves 6 to 8.

Roasted Chicken Breasts with Lemon, Fresh Herbs and Garlic

6 large chicken breast halves, on bone and skin
12 lemons, thinly sliced
12 fresh sage leaves
6 fresh thyme sprigs
6 fresh rosemary sprigs
Filippo Berio olive oil
juice from 1 large fresh lemon, seeds removed
1 small garlic head, sliced
1½ cups fresh chicken stock

To roast the chicken: Loosen the skin from the chicken with your fingers. Slide 2 lemon slices, 2 sage leaves, 1 thyme sprig and 1 rosemary sprig under the skin of each breast. Smooth the skin to close, making sure the skin covers the meat. Season both sides of the breast with salt and pepper. Place the chicken in a large baking dish. Brush each breast with olive oil. Pour the lemon juice over each breast. Add the garlic and 1 cup of chicken stock. Place the dish in a preheated 450 degree oven. Roast for 20 minutes. Baste twice while roasting with the pan juices. Cook until the chicken reaches an internal temperature of 160 degrees. Remove the breasts from the oven.

For the sauce: Remove the chicken from the roasting pan. Place the pan on the stove. Mash the garlic with a spoon. Add the remaining stock. Bring it to a boil. Reduce to a glaze-like consistency. Place the chicken on a platter. Spoon the glaze over the top of each breast. Serve immediately.

Serves 4.

Grilled Pork Chops with Bourbon Mustard Glaze

⅓ cup ketchup
¼ cup bourbon
2 tablespoons whole grain mustard
2 tablespoons light soy sauce or tamari
4 pork rib chops, half-inch thick

For the glaze: Mix all the ingredients — except for the pork — in a saucepan. Bring the mixture to a boil. Reduce at a simmer until the glaze coats a spoon's back.

To grill the pork: Season both sides of the chops with salt and pepper. Brush the glaze onto one side of the chops. Place those sides down on a hot grill. Cook for approximately 4 minutes. Before turning, brush the glaze on top of the pork. Cook for 4 minutes on that side. Remove them from the grill. Serve immediately.

Serves 2.

Grilled Steak Fajitas

2 tablespoons Filippo Berio olive oil
2 tablespoons fresh lime juice
2 tablespoons fresh lemon juice
1 bottle Mexican beer
2 tablespoons tequila
1 jalapeño pepper, minced
1 teaspoon lime zest, grated
1 pound skirt or flank steak, cut crosswise into 1-inch strips
6 large scallions
1 red bell pepper, cut into squares
kosher salt and black pepper to taste
4 flour tortillas

For the marinade: Add the first 7 ingredients into a bowl. Whisk well to blend. Add the beef, scallions and peppers. Allow the marinade to stand refrigerated for 1 hour. Remove it from the refrigerator, skewer the beef on to 2 to 3 metal skewers and then do the same with the vegetables. Season with salt and pepper.

To grill the fajitas: Grill the beef and vegetables on a hot grill. Cook to desired doneness. The vegetables should be slightly charred and tender. Heat the tortillas on the grill, turning them when brown spots appear. Do not burn. Remove the tortillas from the grill. Divide the beef skewers and the vegetable skewers among the 4 tortillas. Roll them. Serve immediately.

Chef's note: Serve the fajitas with grated cheddar or Monterey Jack cheese, sour cream, guacamole and salsa.

Serves 4.

Rambasicci

1 pound ground pork · 1 pound ground beef ·1 pound ground veal
1 pound shallots, diced
½ cup parsley, chopped
1¼ cups Parmigiano-Reggiano cheese
salt and pepper to taste
3 tablespoons butter
¼ cup basil, chopped
15 cabbage leaves
5 cups marinara sauce
½ cup tomatoes, diced
3 cups vegetable stock
1 bunch chives, diced
¼ cup white wine
2 pounds rice, cooked and cooled

For the meat: In a round skillet, heat the butter. Cook the shallots and meats together. When fully cooked, deglaze with the wine. Cook down until almost dry. Add the Parmigiano-Reggiano, basil and parsley as well as the salt and pepper to taste. The mixture should be moist but not too wet. If too dry, add a little vegetable stock.

For the sauce: Mix the marinara and vegetable stock together in a large saucepan. Add the diced tomatoes and chives. Bring to a boil. Remove the saucepan from the heat. The sauce should be the consistency of a thick broth.

For the cabbage: Peel the leaves off one by one. Blanch them in a large pot filled with boiling, salted water for no more than 1 minute. Remove the leaves. Drop them into an ice bath. If the cabbage is still hard — depending on its size — dip the cabbage back into the hot water again. The leaves should fold without cracking.

To stuff the cabbage: Lay the cabbage out flat on a smooth work surface. Place a generous amount of meat and rice mixture in each leaf. Remember that the leaves need to be folded, so don't overstuff each leaf. Place each cabbage in a large baking dish — seam-side down. Cover with the sauce. Bake for 20 to 25 minutes in a 350 degree oven. Serve while hot, with extra sauce and more grated Parmigiano-Reggiano cheese. Enjoy!

Recommended wine:
Prosper Maufoux Puligny-Montrachet (Burgundy, France)

Vegetables

Baby Carrots with Salsify Cream

1 bunch baby carrots
1 bunch baby yellow carrots
1 bunch baby red carrots
4 ounces heavy cream
6 ounces salsify, peeled and diced
1 teaspoon nutmeg
1 teaspoon sugar
chopped chives
to taste white pepper
2 ounces butter

For the carrots: Peel and trim carrots until all uniform. In boiling salted water, blanch carrots shock in ice water and reserve.

For the salsify: In shallow saucepan combine cream, salsify, sugar, nutmeg, cook over low heat until salsify is fork tender transfer to Blend Tec and puree strain through chinois reserve, keep hot.

For the dish: In a sauté pan add butter and carrots cook for three minutes add salsify cream, and chives.

Chefs Tip: After peeling salsify reserve in cold water with lemon juice to prevent from turning brown.

Broccoli and Cheddar Casserole

2 pounds broccoli florets
1 pound cheddar cheese, shredded
8 ounces butter
1 pound butter crackers (Ritz), broken

For the casserole: In a five quart saucepan bring three quarts of salted water to a boil add broccoli cook for five minutes strain, reserve. In a mixing bowl toss crackers broccoli and cheese spread evenly in an oven safe glass baking dish, top with dollops of butter over casserole bake 10 minutes at 375 degrees.

This recipe was given to me by a friend from culinary school's mother, try it with any roasted beef dish you'll love it.

Broccoli Mousse

1 pound broccoli, cooked and pureed
4 eggs
2 yolks
4 ounces heavy cream
2 ounces sour cream
Salt
white pepper

For the mousse: Whip all the ingredients in a mixing bowl until smooth. Transfer to six ramekins bake in a water bath for 20-25 minutes at 325 degrees.

Chefs tip: When cooking in a water bath always place the ramekins in the pan then place in the oven, after that bring the water in a pitcher over to the oven this will prevent water from spilling.

Honey and Ancho Pepper Glazed Corn

6 ears of corn
1 cup honey
3 ounces ancho pepper
1 teaspoon salt
1 teaspoon coriander
1 teaspoon garlic salt
4 ounces Fellipo Berrio light oil

For the Glaze: In a mixing bowl, combine all the ingredients except the corn.

For the corn: Brush the corn with the glaze. Wrap the corn in aluminum foil. Roast slowly in the oven for 30 minutes at 375 degrees.

This is a great twist on a summertime favorite; try it at your next barbeque!

Lentils with Japanese Eggplant and Porcini Mushrooms

6 ounces Beluga lentils
4 ounces Fillipo Berrio olive oil
2 cloves garlic, crushed
1 onion, diced
2 Japanese eggplant, diced
4 ounces Porcini mushrooms, cleaned and sliced
4 ounces mushroom jus
2 ounces Fetzer Barrel select chardonnay
2 ounces butter

For the lentils: Cook the lentils, in enough water to cover them, place a piece of parchment paper on top to keep submerged, about a half hour or until tender.

For the dish: In a heavy bottom sauté pan, add the oil and garlic, cook until golden add onion. Sweat the onion until translucent, add mushrooms cook well about ten minutes, add eggplant cook until soft. Deglaze with chardonnay reduce by half add mushroom jus bring to a boil season with salt and pepper. Finish the dish by adding the cooked lentils and butter.

Chefs tip: It is very important to add the vegetables in certain steps to ensure extracting all the flavors. This dish is great as a side or on its own.

Roasted Tomato and Garbanzo Beans

6 plum tomatoes
2 cloves garlic, sliced
½ cup basil, chiffonade
8 ounces garbanzo beans, cooked and chilled
4 ounces Reggiano cheese, shredded
4 ounces Fillipo Berrio olive oil
1 teaspoon crushed red pepper
4 ounces tomato juice

For the tomatoes: Quarter the tomatoes, tossing in a bowl with the garlic, basil, red pepper and half the olive oil. On a sheet pan skin side down, roast tomatoes at 275 for one hour.

For the dish: Immediately after tomatoes are taken out of the oven, toss with the beans, and cheese. In a sauté pan, bring the juice and remaining oil mixture to a boil. Combine the tomates with the juice and oil mixture. Serve immediately.

A slice of rustic bread makes the perfect lunch on a cold day.

Spinach Blinis

1 pound spinach, blanched and chopped
6 ounces potato cooked
5 egg yolks
2 eggs
8 ounces flour, sifted
1 teaspoon sugar
1 tablespoon salt

For the Batter: Rice the cooked potato, add the spinach stir in until smooth. Add the eggs and yolks stirring continuously. Stir in all the dry products. It is very important in the recipe to work quickly while the potato is still hot. After the ingredients are mixed chill the batter for one hour.

For the Blinis: In a non-stick pan over low heat add a tablespoon of the batter when the edge of the blini is brown flip and cook on opposite side for one minute.

Chefs tip: When cleaning a non-stick pan never use soap or anything abrasive just run under hot water and wipe out with a clean rag.

Spiced Carrot Custard

1 pint heavy cream
6 egg yolks
2 eggs
2 carrots, peeled and diced
3 teaspoons allspice
1 teaspoon cinnamon
1 teaspoon brown sugar
¼ teaspoon black pepper

For the Batter: Cook the diced carrots in the heavy cream until fork tender. Transfer to Blend-Tec puree until smooth. Add the remaining ingredients, strain through a chinois. Divide batter among six-oven proof ramekins bake in a water bath for 20-25 minutes at 350 degrees.
Chill; custards will last for 2 days in refrigerator.

Chefs tip: Serve as a dessert with whip cream and sugar cookies or as an appetizer with grilled shrimp.

Sweat Pea Wasabi Dip

2 cups frozen peas
4 ounces fresh horseradish
1 teaspoon white pepper
1 cup Japanese bread crumbs

For the wasabi: In a Blend-Tec, combine all the ingriedients and reserve. Cover with plastic wrap in the refrigerator until prior to being served. Crackers, toast points, julienned vegetables, steamed, and fried dumplings all go well with this dip.

Sweet and Spicy Onions

4 large onions
1 cup balsamic vinegar
2 teaspoons crushed red pepper
3 ounces sugar
4 ounces butter

For the dish: Slice the onions very thin. In a heavy bottom sauce pan sauté the onions in butter. To caramelize the onions, cook over low heat for 30 minutes and add the balsamic vinegar, sugar and red pepper. Cook until all the liquid is gone.

This dish is very simple but has so many flavors. In my restaurants we serve this with grilled veal chops. This will compliment any meat.

Portobello Mushroom Veggie Cheeseburger

12 large portobello mushrooms, stems removed and caps cleaned
6 red peppers · 6 yellow peppers · 6 green peppers
1 large zucchini, cut diagonally into 12 slices
1 yellow squash, cut diagonally into 12 slices
1 neon or Japanese eggplant, cut diagonally into 12 slices
10 ounces goat cheese, cut into 12 pieces
1 cup balsamic vinegar · ½ cup Filippo Berio olive oil
kosher salt and black pepper to taste

For the peppers: Coat the peppers with olive oil, salt and pepper. Place them on a baking sheet. Put the sheets into a preheated 475 degree oven. Turn the peppers often. When the skin is completely charred, remove the sheets. Place the peppers in a bowl covered with plastic wrap. Remove the peppers after 10 minutes. Peel the skin off. Cut each pepper in half. Remove the seeds. Put the peppers aside until you're ready to assemble the burger.

For the mushrooms: Mix olive oil and balsamic vinegar together. Season with salt and pepper. Pour the mixture over both sides of the mushrooms. Let them stand for 5 minutes. Place the mushrooms on a hot grill. Cook on both sides until the caps are softened but not limp. Remove them from the grill.

For the squashes: Place the squashes and eggplant in a bowl. Season with salt and pepper. Coat with olive oil. Grill both sides on a hot grill. Do not overcook. The vegetables should have some firmness left. Remove the vegetables from the grill.

To assemble the burger: The mushroom caps will act as the "bun." Spread 1 slice of goat cheese on each mushroom. Start with the red pepper on 1 mushroom cap for the bottom. Alternate the squashes and peppers, using 2 slices of each vegetable on 6 of the mushrooms. Top with the remaining mushroom cap for the top "bun."

For the plate: Cut each burger in half. Place each on a separate plate. Spread the burger so that the burger's middle is visible. Serve with a mesclun greens salad.

Serves 6.

Recommended wines:
Fetzer Eagle Peak Merlot (Mendocino County, California, USA)
Jerry Garcia (Sonoma County, California, USA)

Vegetable Ragout

1 tablespoon Filippo Berio olive oil
1 medium onion, chopped
1 red or yellow bell pepper, cored, seeded and chopped
2 celery stalks, sliced
2 large carrots, sliced
1 cup green beans, cut into 1-inch pieces
1½ cups cherry tomatoes, cut in half
1 cup fresh or frouncesen peas
1 cup marinated artichoke hearts
2 garlic cloves, peeled and chopped
1 tablespoon fresh basil, chopped
¾ cup vegetable stock
1 cup baby spinach leaves, shredded

For the stew: Heat the oil in a large cast-iron pan. Add the onion, pepper, celery, carrots and beans. Cook on medium heat until the vegetables are al dente. Add the tomatoes, peas, artichokes, garlic and basil. Add the stock. Bring it to a simmer. Adjust the seasoning with salt and pepper. Remove the stew from the heat. Toss in the spinach. Serve immediately.

Serves 4.

Desserts

Wine Cookies

1½ cups white wine
1 teaspoon vanilla extract
1½ cup Filippo Berio olive oil
1½ cup granulated sugar
6½ cups sifted flour
½ cup orange juice
¼ cup Molinari sambuca
½ teaspoon salt
1½ teaspoon cinnamon
1 tablespoon orange zest
10x powdered sugar

For the cookie: In a small mixer, combine the dry ingredients: flour, cinnamon and salt. Add only 1 cup of sugar. Add the orange juice, wine, zest, vanilla extract and olive oil. Mix at low speed. When the dough is not sticky and pulls away from the bowl's sides, it's complete. Take the dough from the bowl. Let it sit out for about 20 minutes. Roll it into 6-inch long logs. Sprinkle the remaining sugar on the dough. Place the dough on a sheet pan tray with a piece of parchment paper. Bake in a preheated oven at 350 degrees for 40 minutes. Stick a fork in the center to make sure that the inside is cooked. Remove it from the oven. Let the cookie let cool. Slice it into half-inch pieces. Place them back on the sheet pan with the parchment paper. Place the sheet pan in the oven on 410 degrees for 10 minutes or until golden brown. The purpose for putting them back in the oven is to completely dry them out so that the cookie is crunchy. Sprinkle with powdered sugar.

Chef's note: Serve with Muscat wine.

Recommended wine:
Any 10-year-old ruby port.

Strawberry Zabaglione Shortcake

2½ cups all-purpose flour
2 teaspoons baking powder
½ teaspoon baking soda
½ teaspoon salt
3 tablespoons sugar
6 tablespoons unsalted butter
1 cup buttermilk
6 egg yolks · ½ cup sugar
1 cup Marsala wine
1 pint strawberries
2 cups whipped cream

For the shortcake: Mix all the dry ingredients — except for the half-cup of sugar. Sift into a mixing bowl. With your fingers or a pastry cutter, blend in the butter until the mixture is the consistency of wet sand. Add the buttermilk. Blend the mixture with a spoon until a ball can be formed. Pour the mixture from the bowl onto a floured pastry board. If the dough is too wet, add more flour as needed, but do not overblend. With a floured rolling pin, roll the dough out to a thickness of approximately a half-inch. Use a floured 4-inch round cookie cutter to cut 8 rounds. Brush the rounds with melted butter or buttermilk. Sprinkle them lightly with sugar. Place them on a greased baking sheet. Bake in a preheated 425 degree oven for 10 to 12 minutes or until golden brown. Remove the shortcakes from the oven. They can be warm or cold.

For the zabaglione: Whisk the egg yolks and sugar in a double boiler on a fast simmer. Work quickly so as to not scramble the eggs. When the mixture starts to thicken, add the Marsala wine in a steady stream while continuing to whisk until the mixture has more than doubled in volume and is a smooth consistency.

For the plate: Slice the shortcakes in half. Place them on individual plates. Place sliced strawberries on the bottom half. Spoon the zabaglione while still warm on top of the strawberries. Place the top half of the shortcake at an angle on top of the strawberries. Garnish with fresh mint leaves.

Serves 8.

Recommended drinks:
Dessert wines:
Chateau St. Michel Late Harvest Riesling 1998 (Columbia Valley, Washington, USA)
Rosa Regale Brachetto D'acqui 2002 (Italy)

Strawberry Rhubarb Crisp

2 pounds rhubarb, cut into 1-inch pieces
1 pint fresh strawberries, tops removed and cut in half lengthwise
1 teaspoon vanilla extract
1 teaspoon cinnamon · ¼ teaspoon nutmeg
1 teaspoon lemon zest · ¾ cup sugar
2 cups all-purpose flour · 1½ cups brown sugar
1 cup oats · 1 cup unsalted butter

For the filling: Cut the rhubarb into small 1-inch pieces. Make sure that the rhubarb leaves have been completely trimmed off, as they are inedible. Add the sliced strawberries, vanilla, cinnamon, nutmeg, lemon zest and sugar. Mix well. Pour the fruit mixture into a baking dish.

For the topping: In a bowl, combine the flour, brown sugar, oats and unsalted butter. Using your hands, blend the ingredients together to form large crumbs. Sprinkle the crumb mixture on top of the fruit. Place in a preheated oven at 350 degrees. Bake until golden brown and the fruit is soft (about 30 to 45 minutes). If the top browns before the fruit is cooked, cover with aluminum foil and then lower the temperature to 300 degrees.

For the plate: The crisp is best served warm. Place the slices on plates. Garnish with fresh strawberries and good-quality vanilla ice cream. The crisp can also be garnished with brandy or whipped cream.

Garnish suggestions:
Ice cream
Sorbet
Serves 6.

Recommended drinks:
Appleton Extra 12-year-old rum (Jamaican) in a snifter glass

Jamaican Rum Cappuccino:

1½ ounces Coruba dark rum
1 teaspoon sugar
hot coffee · steamed milk
ground cinnamon
whipped cream

Combine the rum and sugar in a glass. Add equal parts coffee and milk. Top the drink with whipped cream and cinnamon.

Lavender Honey Sabayon

3 teaspoons lavender honey
¾ cup heavy cream
4 egg yolks
2 tablespoons granulated sugar
⅓ cup Marsala wine
3 strawberries, cleaned and quartered

For the whipped cream: In a stand mixer on low speed, add the cream into the bowl. Begin with the whip attachment until the cream starts to form soft peaks.

For the sabayon: Fill a double boiler's bottom halfway with water. Add the top piece. When the water starts to simmer, add the yolks to the pot. Whisk together the sugar, wine, honey and yolks until they start to thicken (about 4 minutes). When the mixture is ready, it should coat a spoon's back and not drip off. Remove the top piece of the double boiler. Place it on top of an ice bath so that just the pot's bottom touches the ice. Continue whisking the yolks until they cool down. Fold the whipped cream into the eggs using a rubber spatula. Cover to refrigerate for 2 to 3 hours. Add the strawberries on top when you plan to serve the dessert. Typically, the sabayon will last 36 hours without it losing its fluff. However, use it as quickly as possible.

Chef's note: Serve the sabayon in a chilled champagne glass, alternating the fruit and mixture throughout the glass.

Recommended drinks (sweets to have with sweets):
Jackson-Triggs Gewürztraminer ice wine
Grand Reserve 2002 (Toronto, Canada)

Korbel Mango Bellini:

1½ ounces mango puree
2½ ounces Korbel Brut
½ ounce Finlandia mango vodka
½ Tuaca orange liquor

Put the mango puree in the bottom of a mixing glass without ice. Pour in the sparkling wine. Don't stir briskly or shake. Gently stir. Strain the drink into a champagne flute pre-rimmed with cocktail candy (mango sugar). Float the liquor on top.

Jelly Donuts Anyone?

1 cup milk · ¼ cup buttermilk
1 teaspoon butter · 1 cup granulated sugar
3 teaspoons dry yeast · 2½ tablespoons warm water
¼ teaspoon 10x sugar · 4 cups all-purpose flour, sifted
3 brown organic eggs · 1 cup blackberry jelly*
1 gallon Filippo Berio olive oil for frying

For the dairy: In a small pot, bring the milk to a boil. Add the butter. Set the mixture aside in a small mixer to cool.

For the yeast: Dissolve the dry yeast with the warm water. Wait for 10 minutes.

For the donuts: Place the 3 cups of flour, granulated sugar, butter, buttermilk and yeast in a mixer on low speed. Add 4 tablespoons of oil to the mixture, along with the eggs. The dough should scrape away from the bowl's sides. If it's too sticky, add a little flour. Add the remainder of flour onto a wooden surface. Place the dough onto the floured surface. Knead the dough until you can roll it into a ball. Lightly sprinkle some flour in a bowl to place the dough in it. Sprinkle some flour on top as well. Cover with plastic wrap. Let it double in size for about 60 to 90 minutes.

For the preparation: When the dough has doubled in size, roll it out onto a floured worktable. Start to roll the dough out to a half-inch thickness. With a round cookie cutter, cut circles in the dough. Place some jam in the dough's middle. Add another round dough circle on top of the jelly, making sure that the dough is even and ready to be closed. Lightly brush the donut's inside edges with water before pinching the ends closed. Lightly flour a sheet pan to place the donuts on it. Let the donuts proof for another 10 minutes with a piece of plastic covering them. Heat the oil to 375 degrees in a deep fryer. Place each donut in the oil — to cook both sides — for at least 2 minutes.

Chef's note: Use a metal spider to work with the donuts in the oil. Sprinkle with powdered sugar

*If you do not have blackberry, you can substitute another flavor of jelly

Recommended drink:

Jumping Jelly Bean:

1 ounce Don Edwardo silver tequila
1 ounce Tuaca liquor
1 ounce fresh lemon juice
chilled Korbel champagne

Shake the tequila, Tuaca and lemon juice. Strain the mixture into a martini glass. Fill the glass with champagne before serving.

White Chocolate Raspberry Crème Brûlée

4 ounces good-quality white chocolate
3 cups heavy cream
1 vanilla bean, split in half
6 egg yolks
3 tablespoons sugar
1 pint raspberries
1 cup light brown sugar

For the custard: Melt the white chocolate in a double boiler. Keep it warm. In a heavy saucepan, bring the cream to a boil with the vanilla bean. Remove the saucepan from the heat. Let it set for 15 minutes to infuse the cream with the vanilla. Remove the vanilla bean. Scrape out the seeds from the pod to mix them into the cream. In a separate bowl, beat the egg yolks and sugar together until the eggs thicken. Slowly add the warm cream, mixing constantly so as to not scramble the eggs. Return the mixture to the heavy saucepan. Cook it over low heat for a few moments. Slowly add the melted white chocolate, mixing well. When the mixture coats a spoon's back, it's done.

To bake the custard: Place an even amount of raspberries in the bottom of 4 shallow custard molds. Place the molds in a baking dish. Slowly fill the dish with water until it reaches halfway up the custard molds. Pour the cream mixture into the molds. Place the baking dish into a preheated 350 degree oven for 15 to 20 minutes or until the custard sets. Do not brown. Remove the pan from oven. Let it cool. Refrigerate the custard until ready to use.

For the plate: Sprinkle an even coating of brown sugar on each custard. Melt the sugar under the broiler in your oven or use a portable propane torch. The sugar should form a hard shell over the custard. Serve garnished with fresh raspberries.

Serves 4.

Recommended drink:
Raspberry Martini:
1 part Godiva liquor
1 part Absolut vodka
splash of Chambord liqueur

Combine with ice, shake well and then serve in glass rimmed with berry sugar from cocktail candy.

Ice Espresso Gilba

2½ cups espresso
4 tablespoons granulated sugar
1 teaspoon coffee liquor

For the espresso: Brew the espresso short to make the coffee as strong as you can make it. In a small pot, bring the coffee to a simmer. Add the sugar to it, constantly stirring. Take the hot liquid, pour it into an ice cube tray and then put it in the freezer. Freeze the tray for about 6 hours or until solid. Place the frozen cubes in a Blendtec blender. Pulse the blender on and off to create broken ice, not slush. Pour the crushed espresso ice in a glass. Drizzle the coffee liquor over the top.

Chef's note: I like vanilla whipped cream on top of this easy dessert. It coats the palate quite well.

Simply-Chocolate Chocolate Chip Cookies

3¼ cups all-purpose flour, sifted
1¼ cup butter
¼ cup margarine
1½ teaspoons baking powder
1¾ cups dark brown sugar
1 teaspoon salt
1 cup granulated sugar
4 brown organic eggs
2 teaspoons vanilla extract
2 cups sweet chocolate chips
3 chocolate wafer bars, chopped
1 8-ounce dark chocolate bar, diced

For the mix: In a small bowl, combine the flour, baking powder and salt. In a small bowl with the electric mixer, combine the butter, vanilla extract and margarine on low speed. Gradually add the sugars. Bring the speed up to high. Stop once to scrape the bowl. Return the speed to low. Add one egg in at a time. When everything is mixed together and there are no lumps, stop the machine. With a rubber spatula, fold in the chocolate chips, chocolate wafer bars and dark chocolate.

For the cooking: With a tablespoon, spoon the cookie batter onto a half-sheet pan lined with parchment paper. Preheat the oven to 365 degrees. Bake for 16 minutes or until golden brown.

Chef's note: Do not remove the cookies from the pan when they are very hot. Let them cool down.

Recommended wines:
18-year-old Glenmorangie scotch
Woodford Reserve small-batch bourbon

Brian Fish
Exec. Pastry

Poached Pears with Ricotta and Mascarpone

4 large pears, peeled, cored and cut in half lengthwise
3½ cups Marsala wine
1½ cups water
1 cinnamon stick
3 whole cloves
1 cup ricotta
1 cup mascarpone
1 teaspoon lemon zest, grated
1 teaspoon lime zest, grated
1 teaspoon orange zest, grated
1 teaspoon vanilla extract
¼ cup honey
¼ cup golden raisins
2 ounces pistachios, chopped
2 ounces almonds, sliced

To poach the pears: Put the Marsala wine, water, cinnamon stick and cloves in a saucepan. Bring the mixture to a boil. Reduce to a simmer. Add the pears to the mixture, placing them facedown. Simmer the pears in the liquid until soft but not mushy (about 15 to 20 minutes). Remove them from the pot. Allow the pears to cool before refrigerating.

For the filling: Combine the ricotta and mascarpone in a mixing bowl. With a hand mixer, mix well. Add all the grated zests, vanilla and honey. Mix until well blended and smooth in consistency. Fold the pistachios in by hand. Refrigerate until ready to serve.

For the plate: With a paring knife, trim a small piece off the bottom of each pear so that it will sit flat on the plate. Spoon a generous portion of ricotta mixture into each pear. Sprinkle the sliced almonds on top of each pear.

Recommended wine:
Taz Pinot Gris 2002 (Santa Barbara County, California, USA)

Brownies

2 sticks unsalted butter
8 ounces good-quality bittersweet chocolate
1¼ cups all-purpose flour
1 teaspoon baking powder
2 cups sugar
4 large eggs
2 teaspoons vanilla
5 ounces walnut pieces, chopped

For the batter: Melt the butter and the chocolate in a stainless steel bowl over a saucepan of simmering water. Stir well to blend. When smooth, remove the saucepan from the heat. In a separate bowl, sift together the flour, baking soda and salt. In another large bowl, whisk together the sugar, eggs and vanilla. Blend until smooth. Slowly whisk the chocolate mixture into the egg mixture. Combine well. Whisk in the flour, blending well. Stir in the walnuts.

To bake the brownies: Grease a 9-inch square baking pan with butter. Line the bottom and sides with parchment paper. Lightly grease the paper. Pour the batter into the pan, and with a spatula, smooth the top of the batter. Place in a preheated 350 degree oven for approximately 35 minutes. The top should have a shine. The sides should be slightly pulling away from the pan. If a more cake-like brownie is desired, continue cooking for another 15 minutes. Remove from the brownies from the oven. Allow them to cool.

Chef's note: The brownies can be served warm or cold. If serving as a plated dessert, a dollop of vanilla ice cream or whipped cream makes this perfect

Chocolate Pots de Crème

2 cups heavy whipping cream
½ cup whole milk
6 ounces good-quality bittersweet chocolate
6 large egg yolks
⅓ cup sugar

For the cream: In a heavy saucepan, bring the milk to a simmer over medium heat. Remove it from the heat. Add the chocolate while whisking to achieve a smooth texture. In a large bowl, whisk the egg yolks and the sugar together, blending well. Slowly add the chocolate mixture while whisking. Be careful not to scramble the eggs. Strain the mixture into another bowl. Allow it to cool for 10 minutes. Skim any foam that develops on the top.

To bake the crème: Pour the cream into 6 small ramekins or soufflé dishes. Cover each with foil. Place the cups in a large baking dish. Add enough hot water to the pan to come halfway up the sides of the cups. Bake in a 325 degree oven for about 1 hour — or until the custard has set and the center moves slightly. Remove the ramekins from the water bath. Remove the foil. Chill until cold. Serve with whipped cream.

Serves 6.

Black and White Cookies

1¼ cups all-purpose flour
½ teaspoon baking soda
½ teaspoon salt
⅓ cup buttermilk
½ teaspoon vanilla
⅓ cup unsalted butter, softened
½ cup granulated sugar
1 large egg
1½ cups confectioner's sugar
1 tablespoon light corn syrup
2 teaspoons fresh lemon juice
¼ teaspoon vanilla
2 tablespoons water
¼ cup unsweetened cocoa powder

For the cookies: In a large bowl, sift together the flour, baking soda and salt. In a separate bowl, mix the buttermilk and the vanilla together. In a stand mixer, beat the sugar and butter together until fluffy. Add the egg. Beat until well mixed. On low speed, alternately add the flour mixture and the buttermilk mixture — beginning and ending with the flour mixture. Scrape down the bowl. Mix until smooth. Spoon ¼ cup of batter about 2 inches apart on a buttered baking sheet. Bake in a preheated 350 degree oven until the tops are puffed up and lightly golden (approximately 15 minutes). Remove them from the pan. Place them on a cooling rack.

For the icings: Stir together confectioner's sugar, corn syrup, lemon juice, vanilla and 1 tablespoon of water in a small bowl. Mix until very smooth. Place half the icing in another bowl. Stir in the cocoa — and add more water if necessary — until the consistency is the same as the white icing.

To ice the cookies: The cookies must be completely cooled before icing them. Use the cookie's flat side for the icing. Spread the white icing over half the cookie. Spread the chocolate icing over the other half.

Yields 10 cookies.

Chocolate Bread Pudding

½ stick unsalted butter
4 cups day-old, country-style white bread, cut into 1-inch cubes
3 ounces unsweetened chocolate, chopped
1¾ cups whole milk
3 large egg yolks
¾ cup sugar

For the pudding: Melt the butter in a large pan. Toss it with the bread. In a saucepan, bring the cream and the milk to a simmer. Remove the mixture from the heat. Place the chocolate in a mixing bowl. Add the cream. Whisk until smooth. Add the yolks and the sugar. Whisk well. Pour the mixture over the bread. Let it stand covered for 1 hour.

To bake the pudding: Butter an 8-inch square pan. Pour the pudding into the pan. Bake in a preheated 350 degree oven until the pudding is just set (approximately 25 minutes). Serve the pudding warm or at room temperature.

Chef's note: Whipped cream or vanilla ice cream goes great with this pudding.

Sambuca Pots de Crème

1½ cups heavy cream
6 tablespoons granulated sugar
4 6-ounce ramekins
¼ tablespoon salt
4 large egg yolks
1 vanilla bean
5 ounces Molinari sambuca

For the custard: Preheat the oven to 300 degrees. In a saucepan over medium heat, scald the cream, sugar and salt. Remove the mixture from the heat. In a separate 2-quart saucepan over medium heat, cook the sambuca until it's reduced by half. Remove the saucepan from the heat. Carefully add the scalded cream mixture to the sambuca, constantly whisking until combined. Whisk together the yolks and vanilla in a mixing bowl. Add the cream and sambuca mixture, taking care to temper the cream and eggs. Strain the mixture through a fine mesh strainer into a 1-quart glass measuring cup. Skim off any foam with a spoon. Divide between ramekins. Arrange in small roasting pan. Bake in a water bath until they are firm around the edges but tremble slightly in the middle.

For the dish: Fresh berries, whipped cream or vanilla sauce would all go great, but I prefer to use something with some texture. In my restaurant, I use espresso biscotti, but any coffee-flavored cookie will work.

Chef's note: When baking in a water bath, place a rag at the roasting pan's bottom before filling the ramekins. After pouring water into the pan, the rag will prevent the ramekins from slipping.

Recommended drink: Fill a pony glass three-fourths full with Molinari sambuca, adding a little vanilla bean.

Chocolate Marquis with Grand Marnier

3 cups heavy cream
12 ounces melted bittersweet chocolate
1 cup Grand Marnier liqueur, reduced by half
1 cup 10x confectioner's sugar

For the cream: In a stand mixer, whip the cream and the 10x sugar until soft peaks form. Transfer the cream into a stainless steel bowl.

For the chocolate: In a double boiler, melt the chocolate until there are no visible lumps.

For the Grand Marnier: In a pan on medium heat, reduce the liqueur by half.

To assemble: Adding the Grand Marnier last, combine and fold all the ingredients. Chill for 3 hours. Spoon the marquis into large wine glasses. Garnish with fresh berries or candied orange rind.

Recommended drink:
Grand Marnier's Cuvee du Centcinquantenaire 150th Anniversary (a blend of xo and older cognacs) (France)

Butter Cookie Recipe

4 eggs, separated
½ cup plus 2 tablespoons superfine sugar
¼ teaspoon salt
¾ cup flour, triple-sifted
1 teaspoon vanilla extract
6 tablespoons melted butter, warm

For the dough: Beat the egg yolks in a bowl with a wire whisk, gradually adding the one-third cup of sugar. Beat until thick and lemon-colored. Beat the whites in another bowl with the salt until soft peaks form. Gradually add the remaining sugar to the egg whites, beating thoroughly after each addition. Sift the flour into the yolk mixture. Fold in the beaten egg whites slowly. Slowly fold in the butter vanilla. All these operations must be performed with speed and care or the recipe will collapse. Grease a large baking sheet. Sprinkle flour over it. Drop each teaspoon of batter 2 inches apart. Bake about 8 to 10 minutes in a 325 degree oven until the edges turn brown. Remove the cookies from the baking sheet. Allow them to cool before serving.

For the plate: Butter cookies are a basic cookie that can be used during all holiday seasons. By adding different-colored sugars, it changes the cookie's theme. Try dipping them in tempered chocolate after baking.

Basic Cheesecake

2½ packages cream cheese, 8 ounces each and softened
1¼ sticks unsalted butter (softened) plus butter to line the pan
1½ cups sugar
8 large eggs, separated
2 teaspoons fresh lemon zest, finely grated
2 tablespoons fresh lemon juice
1 teaspoon vanilla
½ teaspoon orange flower water
½ teaspoon almond extract
¼ cup cornstarch

Special equipment needed: A 10-inch springform pan and parchment paper cut into a 10-inch round and a 32-inch by 5-inch strip.

For the batter: In a stand mixer, beat together the cream cheese, butter, three-fourths of a cup of sugar, egg yolks, zest, juice, orange flower water and almond extract on medium speed until creamy. Add the cornstarch. Mix on low until combined. In a separate bowl, beat the egg whites on medium speed until they have soft peaks. Add the remaining sugar a tablespoon at a time while beating. Increase the speed to high to achieve stiff, glossy peaks. Fold in the egg whites slowly and gently until mixed thoroughly.

To bake the cheesecake: Butter the springform pan thoroughly. Line the bottom with the circle of parchment. Place the strip against the sides. Line the pan's outside with foil, making sure to cover the pan well. Place the pan into a baking dish that has been filled three-fourths with water. Pour the batter into the springform. Smooth the top out lightly. Place the pan into the center of a 350 degree oven for 55 to 60 minutes or until the top is golden and the cake is firm. Place the pan on a rack to cool completely. Refrigerate for at least 6 hours. Carefully remove the cheesecake from the springform pan, before serving.

For the plate: This cake can be served with fresh fruit or any flavored topping.

Simple Pie Pastry

1½ cups all-purpose flour, unbleached
1½ tablespoons sugar
¼ teaspoon salt
1 stick unsalted butter, well chilled and cut into cubes
1 large egg yolk
1½ tablespoon ice water

To make the dough: Blend the first 3 ingredients in a food processor. Add the butter. Pulse the machine until the mixture forms coarse crumbs. Whisk the egg yolk and ice water together. Add them to the processor. Pulse the mixture until the dough forms a ball. Add more water if necessary. Remove the mixture from the bowl. Cover it with plastic wrap. Refrigerate for 1 hour before using. Let the dough rest slightly before rolling.

Chef's note: This dough can be used for any type of pie.

Sugared Walnuts

2 cups granulated sugar
2 cups of walnut halves
2 tablespoons white corn syrup

For the Walnuts: Place the nuts in a 350 degree oven to heat while the sugar is melting. Be careful that the nuts do not burn.

For the Sugar: Place the sugar and the corn syrup in a heavy skillet over a low flame. As soon as the sugar begins to turn light brown, tilt the pan in all directions to distribute the heat evenly. As soon as the sugar turns an amber color, remove the nuts from the oven and dump them in. Poke mixture with a wooden spoon. Pour the sugar on a Silpat® (nonstick sheet pan liner) and add the walnuts over the top. Separate the nuts with 2 forks while the sugar is still, hot move quickly. Let cool for 1½ hours before storing in a sealed container. Keep the container in a cool place away from any humidity.

Useful Definitions

Adjust: The chef must taste before serving and add seasonings.

Agar-agar: Seaweed used as a thickening agent.

Al dente: Italian for "to the tooth;" used to describe a food — usually pasta — that is cooked only until it gives a slight resistance.

All-purpose flour: Made from a blend of high-gluten hard wheat and low-gluten soft wheat.

Aperitif: A cooked — usually sweet — wine taken before a meal to stimulate the appetite.

Appetizer: A small serving of food served before a meal or as the first course.

Au jus: French term for roasted meats, poultry or game served with their natural juices.

Baguette: A long, thin, crisp loaf of French bread.

Baking powder: A mixture of sodium bicarbonate and one or more acids used to leaven baked goods.

Barding: A thin piece of fatty bacon or lard used to cover meat while it roasts.

Basil: An herb and member of the mint family; has soft, shiny, light green leaves, small white flowers and a strong, pungent, peppery flavor.

Batter: A semi-liquid mixture containing flour or another starch used to make cakes and breads.

Beat: To make a mixture smooth and introduce air by a brisk regular motion that lifts the mixture repeatedly; to mix vigorously with a brisk motion with a spoon, fork, eggbeater, etc.

Bisque: A thick, creamy soup usually made from shellfish.

Blanch: To immerse food briefly into boiling water and then plunge it into a cold ice bath.

Blend: To mix two or more ingredients together thoroughly with a fork, beater or blender.

Body: Describes a characteristic of wines; a "full bodied" wine is rich without bitterness.

Bouillon: Clear, delicately seasoned soup usually made from lean beef or chicken stock.

Bouquet garni: A combination of herbs tied in cheesecloth that are used to flavor stocks and stews; removed before serving.

Broil: Most ovens have a broiler section that is used to cook meats, fish and poultry or melt or brown foods.

Brunoise: Finely diced or shredded vegetables — usually cooked in butter or stock — used to flavor soups and sauces.

Canapés: Garnished, bite-sized rounds, squares or triangles of bread or vegetables (cucumber, zucchini, etc.) served with cocktails and at buffets.

Caviar: Sturgeon roe.

Cherrystone clam: A clam that is 3-inches long.

Chicken: One of the principal USDA-recognized kinds of poultry; any of several varieties of common domestic fowl used for food as well as egg production; has light and dark meat.

Chicken, broiler-fryer: A chicken 13 weeks old; has a soft, smooth-textured skin.

Chicken, roaster: A chicken 3 to 5 months old; has a smooth-textured skin.

Chiffonade: Finely cut vegetable strips used to garnish soups; raw or simmered in butter.

Chives: An herb and member of the onion family; also know as Chinese chives or flowering chives.

Coarsely chop: To cut food into small pieces about 3/16-inch long.

Coat: To cover a food completely with an outer "coating" of another food or ingredient.

Cockle: A small mollusk related to the oyster.

Combine: To mix two or more ingredients together.

Compote: Mixed fruit — raw or cooked — usually served in desserts.

Consommé: Clear broth that is made from meat or chicken.

Cool: To allow a food to sit until it's no longer warm to the touch.

Court bouillon: A seasoned broth made with water and meat, fish or vegetables.

Couscous: Small, spherical bits of semolina dough that are rolled, dampened and coated with finer wheat flour.

Cream of tartar: Added to candy and frosting mixtures for a creamier consistency and to egg whites before beating to improve stability and volume.

Crêpes: Very thin pancakes.

Deglaze: To pour hot stock, wine or water on the degreased sediment left in the roasting or frying pan in which meat has cooked; brings the natural flavors left in the pan to the surface.

Demi-glaze: A rich, brown sauce or gravy made by reducing meat stock for a length of time (usually 18 hours).

Dice: To cut food into tiny cubes, usually about one-fourth of an inch.

Dijon: French-prepared mustard made in the Dijon region; it has a clean, sharp, medium-hot flavor, yellow-gray color and creamy texture.

Dissolve: To mix a dry substance with liquid until the dry substance becomes part of the solution.

Drizzle: To sprinkle drops of liquid lightly or pour a very fine stream of liquid over an item.

Entrée: A meal's main course, but originally, it was the second course of many.

Filet mignon: A small cut of beef taken from the end of the fillet; it's very tender.

Finely: Very small, as in finely chopped — but not as small as minced.

Flambé: To flame, using alcohol as the burning agent; flame causes caramelization.

Foie gras: Seasoned livers from geese, duck, chicken or veal made into a pâté.

Fondue: A melted sauce, usually with cheese.

Grate: To reduce a larger piece of food to smaller particles.

Herbs: Any from a large group of annual and perennial plants; usually available fresh and dried.

Hors d'oeuvres: A light food — hot or cold — prepared for small servings and to be eaten before the main meal.

Ice bath: A mixture of ice and water used to rapidly chill a food.

Juice: The liquid released or squeezed from any raw state.

Julienne: To slice food into very thin shreds or strips.

Kahlua: A coffee-flavored liquor.

Knead: To work dough by hand or in a mixer to distribute the ingredients.

Ladle: A utensil with a cup-like bowl and a hooked or pierced handle; available in various sizes.

Lard: Tenderized hog fat used in piecrusts and for deep-frying; to insert strips of fat into meat to keep it moist and add flavor via barding.

Marbled: A term for meat laced with fat; when cooked, marbled meat is juicy and tender, so this is a mark of a high-quality piece.

Marinate: To cover food with a marinade for a specified amount of time before cooking.

Mince: To cut food into pieces smaller than when it's chopped.

Olive oil: Obtained by pressing tree-ripened olives; is graded according to its degree of acidity.

Parchment paper: Heavy, grease-resistant paper used to line cake pans or baking sheets or to wrap foods for baking en papillote.

Peach: A medium-sized stone fruit that has a fuzzy, yellow-red skin.

Pinch: The amount of a dry ingredient that can be held between the thumb and forefinger.

Pint: A unit of volume equal to 16 fluid ounces.

Puree: To process a food into a smooth paste, usually with a blender.

Quart: A measure of volume in the U.S. system equal to 32 fluid ounces; 4 quarts equal 1 gallon.

Rack: A rib section of meat.

Roux: A paste of butter and flour that is used to thicken almost everything.

Sabayon: A sweet egg dessert or sauce, flavored with wine; in Italy, it's called zabaglione.

Sage: An herb native to the Mediterranean region; has soft, slender, slightly furry, gray-green leaves.

Sauté: To brown or cook a food quickly; in French, it means "jump."

Sear: To brown a meat's surface quickly by cooking it in a little fat at a very high heat.

Shallot: An herb with a garlic-onion flavor; smaller and milder than an onion.

Shredded: Slender pieces of food; similar to julienne.

Sift: To pass dry ingredients — such as flour — through a sieve or sifter to remove lumps, to blend or to aerate ingredients.

Simmer: To cook liquid at a temperature just below the boiling point.

Steam: To cook indirectly by setting food on top of boiling water in a covered pot.

Stiff peaks: Egg whites beaten until they are stiff enough to stand on their own.

Thyme: A low-growing herb with small, purple flowers, a slightly lemony flavor and an aroma; used fresh or dried.

Vanilla extract: A vanilla-flavored product made by macerating chopped vanilla beans in a water-alcohol.

Vichyssoise: A cold soup made with leeks, cream and potatoes.

Water bath: It consists of placing a container (bowl, soufflé dish, etc.) of food in a large, shallow pan of warm water that surrounds the food with gentle heat.

Yorkshire pudding: A popover-like pastry cooked in roast beef drippings.

Zabaglione: A rich Italian custard made by beating egg yolks until they are lemon-colored and then adding sugar and Marsala wine.

Zest: The thin, brightly colored, outermost skin layer of citrus fruit that contains flavorful aromatic oils and is removed with a zester.

Taste This Reference Directory

Below are some of the best companies in the food industry.

All-Clad
www.allclad.com

Blendtec
www.blendtec.com

Bone Suckin' Sauce
www.bonesuckinsauce.com

Brazil Gourmet
www.brazilgourmet.com

Blue Q Gum
www.blueq.com

Bolla Wine
www.bolla.com

Buffet Enhancements
www.buffetenhancements.com

Cambro USA
www.cambro.com

Casa DiLisio
www.casadilisio.com

Chef Revival
www.chefrevival.com

Chef's Hat
www.chefs-hat.com

The Chef's Warehouse
www.chefswarehouse.com

Cooking with Chef John
www.cookingwithchefjohn.com

Cuisipro
www.cuisipro.com
Cinders Barbeques
www.cindersbarbecues.com

Comté Cheese
www.comte.com

D'Artagnan
www.dartagnan.com

De Cecco Pasta
www.dececco.it

Dell'Amore Pasta Sauce
www.dellamore.com

Denby Pottery
www.denbypottery.co.uk
www.denbyusa.com

Eden Foods
www.edenfoods.com

Edgecraft
www.edgecraft.com

Fetzer Vineyards
www.fetzer.com

Filippo Berio Olive Oil
www.filippoberio.com

Icelandic Brand Seafood
www.icelandic.com

Idaho Trout Company
www.idahotrout.com

Jeremiah's Pick Coffee
www.jeremiahspick.com

John Boos & Co.
www.johnboos.com

John Wm. Macy's CheeseSticks
www.cheesesticks.com

Korbel Champagne
www.korbel.com

Loacker Cookies
www.loacker.it

Melissa's World Variety Produce
www.melissas.com

Molinari Sambuca
www.molinari.it

Natalie's Orchid Island Juice Company
www.orchidislandjuice.com

Nueske Hillcrest Farms Meat
www.nueske.com

Planet Sugar
www.cocktailcandy.com

Prosciutto di Parma
www.prosciuttodiparma.com/eng/

Parmigiano-Reggiano
www.parmaitaly.com/parmigianok.html

Phillips Foods (the best crabmeat)
www.phillipsfoods.com

Ravenscroft Crystal
www.ravenscroftcrystal.com

Renaissance Farms (infused sea salts)
www.renfarm.com

Roth Käse
www.rothkase.com

Wolf Appliance
www.subzero.com/wolfdefault.asp

Teaosophy
www.teaosophy.com

Thermo Safe
www.thermosafe.com

Tonton Sauce
www.tontonsauce.com

Tortuga Rum Co.
www.tortugaimports.com

Village Craft
www.villagecraft.biz

Voss Water
www.vosswater.com

Wells' Dairy
www.wellsdairy.com

Wüstof Knifes
www.wusthof.com

Testimonials

"Chef Joe Ciminera is an accomplished professional and knows his way around a kitchen. For someone under the age of 35, Chef Joe continues to impress me with his masterful culinary style and fresh approach to haute cuisine. To date, I have not found any other chef who is as thorough, professional and as real as Chef Joe. Truly, this is amazing for someone without pretense. In this book, I am certain that you will be pleasantly surprised and enlightened with his insightfulness!" — Jason Gordon, president of 3 Alliance Enterprises Inc.

"Joseph Ciminera has been keeping my fingers busy writing columns about his works of art for the past 8 years. Readers and foodies will love this cookbook." — Michelle Finestra, European Culinary Council

"Chef Joe is not only a very accomplished chef of traditional cuisine, but he understands and exhibits the true joy, fun and creativity that come from cooking. He understands the importance of marrying wine flavors with food flavors and excels at its execution." — Richard Plutzer, Master Sommelier

"Chef Joe Ciminera's approach to cooking is wonderful and smart. In this book, he has managed to introduce the common person to cooking superbly with no fear! — a great achievement — which shows how insightful and accomplished he is in spite of his young age." — Mario G. Messina, president of MgM Gold Communications

"Chef Joe Ciminera's refreshing approach to the culinary arts will make you want to count the minutes until the "dinner bell." His creations are not only pleasing to the eye but — more importantly — pleasing to the palate as well. Move over, Emeril!" — Dave Scheiber, vice president of marketing for Filippo Berio olive oil

"Chef Joseph has ... certainly decided to put his mark on the culinary world! Smart, refreshingly honest and to the point, he knows his pantry and enjoys playing in it. Solid, down-to-earth techniques by someone who truly loves his art and wants to share his passion. Add this one to the collection, and remember: 'There are no rules in cooking.'" — Kim de la Villefromoy, executive vice president for Chef Revival USA Inc.

"Joseph Ciminera understands the secret of a great chef is to allow the foods to speak for themselves. He is always subtle in his approach to a dish and original in creating the combinations that make every course a delight. His book is a wonderful read and gives the chef in all of us a chance to improve our talents." — Yvette Somekh, national food critic and television producer

"Joe Ciminera cooks with intensity, passion and imagination. This book will illustrate this concept and make you cook with confidence, with curiosity and with a desire to please everyone at your table." — Salvatore Rizzo, event coordinator for the James Beard Foundation and co-inventor of the Spoonless Pasta Bowl

Index